Daughters of The King

Daughters of The King

by Pat Brooks

Creation House
Carol Stream, Illinois

This book is dedicated to
Jesus Christ
who is
King of Kings
and
Lord of Lords

©1975 by Creation House. All rights reserved. Published by Creation House, 499 Gundersen Drive, Carol Stream, Illinois 60187. In Canada: Beacon Distributing Ltd., 104 Consumers Drive, Whitby, Ontario L1N 5T3. Biblical quotations are used with permission from the New American Standard Bible ©1971 by the Lockman Foundation. Printed in the United States of America.

ISBN 0-88419-114-1

Library of Congress Catalog Card Number 75-225-73

CONTENTS

Foreword
Preface

1	What About Sarah?	12
2	My Chat With a Women's Libber	21
3	Finding Our Feminine Role	29
4	The Women's Retreats Are Born	39
5	Encountering God's "Hornets"	48
6	"Letters" Worth Reading	57
7	Launching Our Sons	68
8	Hazards of the End-Time Voyage	78
9	In the Footsteps of Three Mary's	88
10	Doormat or Disciple?	95
11	The Last Beatitude	104
12	Some Awesome Visions	113
13	Deborah? or Jezebel?	122
14	Is God's Way Worth Fighting For?	132
	Bibliography	143

Foreword

Confused young Debbie, Chapter 2, had just been granted at least one moment of significant insight, not attributable to her "gold wire-rimmed glasses" nor clouded by her drug-blown mind. In that instant, turning to Pat Brooks, she said, "I do believe you're real."

As Pat's pastor, I thank God for His divine direction, the "hornets" notwithstanding (chapter 5), which brought this very "real" person, her husband Dick (now an elder in our church) and fine family to Pineview!

Within the confines of the local church, to say nothing of her influence nationally, the ministry of Pat Brooks has been extraordinary. Though not a member of Pineview's staff, she has become an integral part of its body life and ministry. The lives of hundreds have been enriched by her Sunday classes, scores have been set free of satanic bondage at the prayer meetings in the Brooks home, and her earlier books have become a part of the tools of our church's counseling ministry.

Obvious intelligence and talents fail to explain this rare breed of woman. Pat's secret lies in a life which has been baptized with the Spirit of God and endowed by many gifts of the Spirit. But, unlike many who make similar claims today, there is to be found in her life and ministry a profound respect for Biblical authority.

In my judgment, Pat Brooks passes with straight A's her own test of feminine ministry. She has found her "godly feminine role," and in her personal life she likewise wears with grace and humble dignity the royal robes of a "daughter of the King."

The essence of this book is long overdue, and for many "daughters of Eve" and heartsick daughters of the King, it will prove just what the Doctor (Jehovah-Raphah) ordered.

Willard L. Davis, Pastor
Pineview Community Church
Albany, New York

Preface

It is high time for the church to wake up from its long sleep on the subject of the woman's role in a modern, complex society. Subversive groups organize "women's libbers" who picket with militant posters their message of rebellion and anarchy. Yet at the other end of the pendulum swing, thinly disguised male chauvinists reiterate the time-worn half-truth, "woman's place is in the home."

No amount of rhetoric will ever repeal God's Word or His pattern for society and the family. Under God the man is still head of the home, but woman is its heart. The question then, to which this book is addressed, is, *"What do you do for a sick heart?"*

The controversy of our day comes in the grey zone of confusion for enlightened, educated women who do not stop progressing because they are married; who do not stop thinking because they are Christian believers. On this subject the church has maintained a tight-lipped and guilty silence. Into this vacuum where no trumpet even brings forth an uncertain sound, who can prepare himself—or herself—for battle?

This vacuum might prove to be the hurricane center of social revolution in our day. When one out of three marriages ends in divorce, and 10,000 teenagers run away in the United States every week, is not something very, very wrong?

Medical science tells us that the two great killers of our day are cancer and heart disease. If this is true for the physical body, may we not suggest it as a possibility for the family unit, as well?

It is our conviction that the heart disease afflicting modern womanhood is an aching sense of unfulfillment. She has been over-educated for a destiny of underachievement. The era of prepared foods has stolen her motivation to develop the creative arts of baking and gourmet cooking. Home has become a hotel-restaurant for itinerants, rather than a center for settlers. How can she develop the fine art of conversation with a husband and children who spend all noncommitted time in front of a television set?

Perhaps she has a "degree" or even a "masters" in some such field as political science. What on earth does this have to do with a lifetime of "playing house"? What does a woman *do* with the conflict aroused by a clash between training and circumstances? Will it erupt in a sudden "heart attack" such as a suicide, mental breakdown, or divorce? Or might it slowly paralyze her mind and will, leading to a kind of "hardening of the arteries" of caring?

If indifference and apathy take over, she may spend more and more time on the telephone or in front of the television set. Or she may well escape into literary dry rot; even pornography. Finally even the public service announcement at the end of the eleven o'clock news cannot arouse her from her stupor: "Parents, where are *your* teenage children now?"

We ask you, Body of Christ, is she not sick?

Yes, the honest ones will admit, she is sick. So is her husband or father or brother or employer. (Often, he is sick of her!) Often he has fallen prey to the cancer of resentment which eats away at the very essence of his manhood. Yet the subtle ways he conveys his hostile reactions to her only speed up her advancing disease with feelings of rejection.

Did God ever intend for us to be like this? Does He have an answer for our age before it drowns itself in despair? Is His Word relevant for a culture where women are doctors, lawyers, educators, school bus drivers, writers, executives, police women and politicians—as well as homemakers?

Yes! He is calling daughters of Eve all over this world from their morass of deception and futility into a new life of purpose and joy. In these days of getting ready for the Bridegroom He is preparing His bride.

No wonder He has special training these days for children of His royal family. May this book be a sketchy map, at least, for sisters seeking to find the King's Highway on their way to the wedding feast. It will have served its purpose if even one leaves forever behind her stigma and stereotype as a daughter of Eve. But I think there are multitudes just longing to discover all it means to be, in every sense, daughters of the King!

Pat Brooks
Ballston Lake, New York
July, 1975

1 What About Sarah?

Read All about It!
Psychiatrist's wife commits suicide after shooting her husband and children! Women's Lib leader deserts family to take over day care center for children of working mothers! Coed dies in dormitory the day after an abortion! Nude corpse of movie sex symbol found after overdose of drugs!

Read All about It!
A female servant of Jesus Christ succumbs to a nervous breakdown after years of submission to an alcoholic husband. Another commits suicide after two decades of marriage to a homosexual. A third welcomes cancer rather than continued coexistence with a tyrant.

Read All about It!
Christian women declare some current preaching false. Female Bible teachers warn Jesus is Lord, not hubby; male chauvinists challenge their right to teach. Lady artists, beauticians, writers, secretaries, musicians, engineers, teachers, and police women claim their right to work; male authorities say "no go if married!"
READ ALL ABOUT IT!

The problems in lives of believers may not make headlines, but the conflicts are there. Today the church of Jesus Christ faces a dilemma caused by a pendulum swing from rank modern feminism. The screaming "equal rights" party of the radical left has its counterpart in the Body of Christ booming, "no rights." The unique present phenomenon of mothers deserting their families has its tragic backlash in women who are caught in the web of certain false teaching. A pious hammering away on "submission" has brought about chaos in the Body of Christ. What may have started as a healthy return to divine order in the home has become, with some, a cloak for male chauvinism.

The women's libber recognizes no authority or divine order. If she is married, her husband may either become her *enemy* or her *slave*. Rebellion is her root problem, breeding a license which leads to extreme forms of bondage. In her rejection of her feminine role, she is at war with her Creator as well as with His male creatures. She seeks *conquest* in her relationships with men, not concord.

How easy it is for us to recognize such obvious error on the left—and then lurch far over to the right! No wonder Paul warned, "It was for freedom that Christ set us free; therefore keep standing firm and do not be subject again to a yoke of slavery" (Galatians 5:1).

The captive wife who has swallowed false teaching on "submission" is either a *doll* or a *doormat*. Thus it follows that her husband will function in her life either as her *idol* or a *despot*.

If her root problem is idolatry, she has broken the first commandment and is out of close fellowship with God. Thus she tries to fill the void in her heart by possessiveness and jealousy of her husband. She devours teaching like that in a current bestseller giving her novel variations of feminine wiles. More mistress than wife, she is forever trying to lure her idol away from duties with seductive tricks. She may cloak her selfish demands with disarming flattery, but her submission is phony at best. The doll-wife usually has an iron will, trying to manipulate her husband like a wind-up toy.

If the captive wife is a *doormat,* on the other hand, she probably suffers most from subjugation. In seeking to serve as her husband's puppet, her will may be paralyzed to the point of passivity. In this state demonic oppression is inevitable. Just as the doll is chained by selfishness, so the doormat is caught up in hopelessness.

The end result for both women is bondage. They have not so much *rejected* their feminine role, however, as *distorted* it. Either type will resort to *deceiving* men to get what they want.

Is this sawdust the best teaching the body of Christ can give its female servants? Is this the kind of woman of whom God says, *"Strength* and *dignity* are her clothing" (Proverbs 31:25)?

More voices in the church are crying out otherwise, daily. Not long ago I was asked to teach at a women's conference in a Midwestern city where the pastor had begun to recognize very poor fruit resulting from false teaching in his area.

He told me some Bible teachers see themselves as Elijahs before modern Ahabs and Jezebels. They teach an extreme form of submission where the man reigns as dictator in his home. The wife, beneath him, must yield to all his demands, regardless of how unreasonable or sinful.

In that city a network of home fellowships had shared this teaching with a vengeance, demanding compliance. The result was a state of chaos in which many women were depressed and one had committed suicide.

But how the pastor came to invite me to that city is the strangest story of all. He said he had never heard of me nor read any of my books. However, several women from the home groups heard me speak in another city. They went home and asked the elders of their churches to sponsor my coming. They were refused, on the grounds that "I suffer not a woman to teach" (I Timothy 2:12). Then they called the pastor who became my host, begging him to invite me.

"I got off that phone," he told me, "and said, 'This has got to be God! Those women would *never* go against that iron rule of those groups unless there were some motivation stronger than their fear of reprimand from those elders. I've got to get Pat Brooks here!' "

The conference was one attended by a unique blessing from God. His presence was markedly *there,* from the start.

On the last day, during a question period following the morning message, a young woman brought up a piece of paper to me. On it were written the words, "What about oral sex? Should a Christian wife submit to that?"

I waited until a few others had asked questions from the floor, and then read this one out loud.

"No," I said. "No woman needs to submit to sin. If she were allowed to do that, you would have to rewrite the whole Word of God."

"But Pat," one young extrovert said, jumping to her feet. "What about Sarah? Didn't God honor her because she submitted to Abraham, when he lied and let her go into Pharoah's harem?"

"Nonsense!" I answered, glad for the chance to warm up to a favorite subject. "God does not honor sin or obedience to sinful demands. He kept Pharoah from touching Sarah because she was His choice for the direct line of ancestry for His Son, the Messiah."

This time a taller, more sober, girl was speaking. Her face was genuinely troubled, and it was obvious she was not joking.

"But we've been taught by a man under the covering of our home fellowships that we should submit to *any* demand our husbands make, even if it should be wife-swapping."

I ignored the ripple of laughter throughout the room.

"If that were so," I replied, "we would have to annul the whole Word of God. In all our thinking about submission we have to remember our primary yielding is to *Jesus as Lord,* and therefore to *His Word* before any human word. Lord means 'boss.' If Jesus is Boss of my life, then I do what He says. It is just as we teach the children in Sunday School or Bible clubs: 'God said it, I believe it, and that's the end of it.' "

The tall girl persisted. "But aren't we to obey all human authority here on earth, as His chain of command?"

I zeroed in. "Only when it does not violate God's clearly revealed will in the Bible. For instance, I have to obey the traffic laws, for God's Word says so in Romans 13:1—'Let every person be in subjection to the governing authorities.'

"However, if the day should ever come when government authority would seek to make me recant my faith in Jesus Christ, my answer would be the same one Peter gave the Jewish Council: 'We must obey God rather than men' (Acts 5:29). It is on that basis that Brother Andrew conducts his life work and has his powerful message and book, *The Ethics of Smuggling.*"

My tall friend stood her ground. "But how can you apply such reasoning to Sarah? *Twice* she submitted to her husband's demands to enter a heathen harem, and *twice* God protected her!"

I picked up my Bible. "True, but I doubt for the reason you think. If God had wanted Sarah to submit to Abraham even when he was wrong in a moral issue, why did He honor her when she demanded that Ishmael be sent away? Are you going to rip Genesis 21 right out of your Bible?"

There was a fluttering of pages all over the room—one of the sweetest sounds to a Bible teacher's ears. (If we can get to the place where this hunger is there for the Word *all* the time, we'll have an awakening in this nation that will eclipse the present one. Perhaps then God's people will fulfill their rightful roles as *salt* and *light* in this decaying, dark age. *Then* we shall be equipped to lead our nation back to godliness, as our forefathers did in New England when they founded it. What a day that will be!)

"She really told Abraham off, all right," one girl said. "It's natural for a woman to want the best for her son. And after all, she *had* been responsible for the birth of Ishmael. She probably felt guilty about it."

"Never mind how she felt," I said. "There is more than natural feeling involved here. It's a supernatural thing and has to do with the sovereignty of God. He will not allow the life in the flesh to coexist with the life in the Spirit. Ishmael stands for the life in the flesh, since he was born 'by the will of man.' Isaac stands for the life in the Spirit, since he was born through a miracle, according to Galatians 4. Whenever the will of God is involved in some basic way as it is here, we had *better* obey God's Word before any man's word! No husband has the right to annul God's moral or spiritual laws, and a wife who submits to such things is heading toward darkness."

"But how can you apply something like this to oral sex? After all, doesn't the Scripture say, 'Let the marriage bed be undefiled'?" (Hebrews 13:4).

"Yes," I answered. The place had become very still. "But that's not the marriage bed, any more than rectal sex is. The law defines those things loosely under the term, *sodomy,* which is condemned in Scripture. The Bible also says, 'Flee immorality. Every other sin that a man commits is outside the body, but the immoral man sins against his own body' (I Corinthians 6:18). In the Greek the word for immorality is *porneia.* The root here indicates any kind of wrong sexual practice; it's the word we get our word 'pornography' from."

It was time to go. One of the local people closed in prayer, and I thought we had heard the end of that discussion. But to my amazement there were several calls during the day from women who were trying to reconcile perversion under the guise of submission to their husbands. Just before I left that city a woman came to me in obvious torment.

"You have ruined my whole day!" she announced, as she flounced into a chair near mine. "I have been under such conviction since you talked about oral sex. I got so upset I went down to my husband's office and told him what you said, and now he's mad at you, too. We had perfect peace about what we were doing until you came along. I wish you had never come."

"Why? If you have 'perfect peace' about your behavior, should my remarks unsettle you? God's kind of peace is not upset that easily."

"But don't you see that you have done a lot of harm?" she asked me earnestly, leaning over toward me with frightened eyes. "My peace was based on the very Scripture that other girl brought up this morning: 'Let the marriage bed be undefiled.' How dare you say certain practices are not for the marriage bed? Anything that happens between married people in the privacy of their own bedrooms is surely all right."

"We're not going to get very far haggling over that verse," I said. "I suggest you take another approach. Look at Matthew 7:15-18 and then apply the *fruit test* to your life."

I handed her my Bible and she read through the passage impatiently.

"Well?" she asked, her eyes flashing, as she slammed the Bible shut. "What on earth does this have to do with what we are talking about?"

"Let's find out," I answered. "Tell me, how much time do you spend in the Scriptures daily?"

She hung her head.

"I get a headache when I try to read the Bible," she said, squeezing several tissues into a tight wad in her hands.

"Then you don't really dwell on it and put that time first in your day?"

"No," she said reluctantly. "I get very little out of it."

"All right. How about prayer? How much time do you spend

in prayer every day?"

"I try to find time to pray. But I always get *sleepy*. Usually I wake up later and don't even know how long I've been there."

"How long has it been like this in your life?"

"Four or five years."

"How long have you and your husband been practicing oral sex?"

Suddenly her face reddened. She looked over at me, startled.

"About the same amount of time," she whispered.

"Well then, examine the fruit for yourself," I said, shrugging my shoulders. "Do you want the kind of walk you had with God before this started in your life, or the kind you have now? What way do you think is most pleasing to the Lord?"

She did not answer. I did not expect her to. The point had hit home, and a great misery spread over her face. She looked down and rolled the paper wad back and forth between her hands.

"You don't understand," she said finally, in a detached, hoarse voice. "If I don't submit to his wishes in this area I might lose him."

"Is he a Christian?"

"Yes, and a leader in the church. I won't tell you what he does."

"I don't want any details," I said wearily. "But I suspect this is a very big issue between him and the Lord. God says 'Those who honor Me I will honor' (Samuel 2:30). You both have a great responsibility to repent and clean up your lives. You may need deliverance from evil spirits, too. But as his wife, you have the same responsibility Sarah had to stand for God. You cannot ignore the issue now that God has brought it to the light."

"But what if I *lose* him?" she rasped, starting to sob.

"Who's first in your life; your husband or the Lord Jesus Christ?"

She did not answer, but kept sobbing. I happened to have with me a book I had written, *Climb Mount Moriah*. I gave it to her.

"Maybe this will help you to answer that one," I said. "I have to go, now."

She reached her hand out to mine as I got up.

"Thank you for spending time with me," she said. "Please pray for me."

"I will, right now," I said, closing my eyes where I was standing. "Father, clear the confusion from the mind of this dear sister and help both her and her husband to do Your will. I bind every evil spirit which has deceived them, and loose them to do the right thing, in Jesus' name. Amen."

The ride to the airport was lively. There were four of us in the car, and all had been at the morning meeting.

"One gal called me this afternoon and talked with me for a half hour about the question of submitting to perversion," the pastor's wife said. "She's a recent convert and really wants to please the Lord. Evidently she and several friends talked about this whole thing very frankly over lunch and found their husbands were still expecting the same things of them now which they had before."

"Are the husbands Christians too?" I asked.

"Yes, in this case, they are. But what if they were not? What would you say to these women, then?"

"I'd still say the same thing. Should an alcoholic's wife drink with him after she has been converted, to avoid his wrath? Should a believer sign a joint income tax return if her husband has lied, cheated, and is guilty of fraud?"

"I see your point," one of the women from the back seat of the car said. "It's the issue of two wrongs not making a right, again. If submission to the husband forces a believer to disobey God's Word, she cannot do that."

"Exactly. And I know of no case where God has failed to honor such a woman, in her obedience to Him. However, I know of *several* where women have gone into gross darkness and a terribly backslidden condition submitting to husbands who were out of the will of God."

A few weeks later I was riding to the Pittsburgh Airport with two women from a nearby city, where I had just spoken. We were discussing the whole matter of the current controversy over "submission" teaching.

"I have no problem with submission when I am right with the Lord," Al Brady said. "That's always the key matter: being yielded to *Him*. When that's right, all other relationships fall into place."

Suddenly all three of us spotted a woman carrying a five-gallon can of gasoline toward a car parked on the other side of the road. Inside the car a man waited for her, in the driver's seat.

"Did you see *that*?" I said, laughing as we passed the strange scene. "What an example of submission!"

"Oh, come now," Phyliss Smith said, from the back seat, with her soft British accent. "We must be a *wee* bit charitable. Perhaps he has only one leg!"

2 My Chat With a Women's Libber

There she was, scrawny and belligerent, eyeing me through gold, wire-rimmed glasses, as she huddled against the window of the jet. More than blue jeans and a fringed western jacket, she wore a studied scorn for the "establishment" symbols she saw around her. Yet, one glance told me she was wearily stereotyped by her subculture. In that, she was a perfect conformist.

I settled into the aisle seat, frankly glad there was an empty one between us. I had moved from a draftier spot just next to the smokers' section. Twinkling Chicago disappeared beneath the night clouds as I started to read. It was comfortable here, and I was in no mood to talk.

A few minutes later the stewardess served us both Cokes. I could sense the gaze of the straggly blue-jeaned blonde watching me, but she said nothing. Finally either an inner nudging or a mundane curiosity moved me toward conversation. (Her first words spelled that last one, c-o-n-t-r-o-v-e-r-s-y.)

"I'm Pat Brooks. What's your name?"

"Debbie,"

(That figured. They never have last names anymore, if they are under twenty-five.)

"Where are you from, Debbie?"

"Out West."

"Good. I like the West. We used to live out there," I said, glancing at her wedding band. "Your husband's out there?"

"Yup. I'm visiting my father. He's going to take me back to visit my college and a bunch of other places."

"Fine. Where did you go?"

She named a famous university; then told me it was

"significant" to have gone there, but had little bearing on her present life. She was working as a carpenter; her husband at another trade. However, he was waiting for a break in his first-love field of rock music.

Then I asked her the question which set her off like the recording you get at an airline's reservations desk when all the lines are busy.

"What does it mean to you to be a woman in today's society?"

"You mean you call this (expletive deleted) mess men have made of things a *society*?" she hissed, eyes bulging. "It's more like a jungle, where the strong feed on the weak. I identify with the oppressed peoples waiting to be liberated. One day a whole new order will come in, with the women in charge."

"What makes you think they'll do a better job?" I asked, smiling broadly, shifting in my seat to face her.

"The men have never been qualified to lead. They just grabbed power years ago because they were physically stronger and could subdue women. And they've certainly left us some (expletive deleted) here, with people hungry and oppressed, and many never having a chance to rise above their caste level."

"No, that's not completely accurate," I said lightly. "*God gave man authority. He didn't just grab it.*"

"That's not the kind of God I know," she sneered at me.

"Oh, do you know God?" I asked softly. Suddenly there was a "hush" on our conversation. I knew He was right there with us, dealing with her in the way that only He can.

"Yes, I've met Him," she said, lowering her voice and brightening. "Often. When I've been on drugs."

"How can you be sure the one you've met is the right God?" I asked.

"Why are you so suspicious?" She stiffened, glaring at me again. "He's given me some great feelings, I can tell you. The most deeply religious people I know are those on L.S.D. It's a way to tune into the spiritual world, for those with the courage to live that way."

"You call it courage, Debbie, to cop out on life?" I asked, leaning over the seat a little and looking right into those hostile, frightened eyes. I could sense God's love for this girl welling up within me. (This still amazes me, for people hard to *like*.)

"What better way is there, then?" she challenged me. "With this world so fouled up, how can a person have the kind of strength it takes to change it without communicating to a higher world?"

"Ah, now we're getting somewhere," I said shifting back closer to the aisle again. "You're surely right there. This world has no answers. God has them. He loves you and He brought us together tonight, because He does not want you looking for Him on drug trips. He makes a permanent change within so you never need to cop out again."

"How can you be so sure you're right?" she said, her voice wavering slightly.

"Because He changed me eighteen years ago when I was just a little older than you are, and I've never been the same since. Before that I tried to change the things I hated in myself. But no matter what I tried, nothing worked."

"What kind of things?"

"Things like my foul mouth."

That hit home. She was silent for a minute.

"Why do you call God 'He,' anyway?" she asked, with a new burst of annoyance. "How do you know it's not 'she'?"

"Because He says so, here in His Word," I said, tapping my brown leather New American Standard Bible gently. "He never lies."

"How do you know that's His Word?" she sneered condescendingly.

"Because He says so, roughly 3600 times in here, and because I've found everything in here reliable. No question life raises is without an answer in His Word. It's that *authority* which I searched for all my young life when I wanted answers but had no idea where to find them."

"And you'd probably condemn me for the places I look for answers?" she said, her eyes blazing. She reached into her purse and brought out some Tarot cards. She seemed not to hear me as she spread them out on her lap.

"No, not condemn. Just warn," I said aloud. Then inaudibly, "I bind every evil spirit oppressing this girl and holding her in bondage, and command you to loose her, in the name of Jesus Christ."

For a few minutes we sat in silence. She seemed to be concentrating deeply.

"Tell me, Debbie," I finally said. "You obviously have a concern for other people. If a baby were in a burning house next door all alone, would you do your best to get in there and save that child's life?"

"Of course I would. That's a ridiculous question."

"Not so silly after all. *You're* that baby and those Tarot cards and drug trips are part of the fire Satan is using to try to destroy you."

"Oh, so you believe I'm in the hands of Satan, do you? Well, I'll blow your establishment mind and tell you the whole truth. I'm a women's libber-leftist-radical-lesbian, the whole bit."

"So what else is new?"

She turned toward me and gazed intently at me. She saw no shock, and for the first time all evening her guard began to crumble a little.

"The Lord Jesus loves you," I said very softly, not backing off from her intent gaze. "He sent me here to talk to you. He does things like that."

"*So*! You're a Jesus freak!" she said, jubilant that she could finally peg me.

"If it's freakish to have love, joy, and peace as a free gift without human effort, and not need to cop out on life, I plead guilty," I said matter-of-factly.

"Suppose I make the same claim!" she shot at me, defiantly.

"Your lifestyle denies it," I said, grinning at her. "You've just told me of several ways you cop out on life, regularly. A person's not really free until there is nothing he *needs* to escape from. As long as there are things in your life you can't control, but control *you,* you're not free."

Debbie looked down at the Tarot cards on her lap and changed positions of a couple. She seemed to be playing some kind of solitaire.

I opened my Bible and began to read. Before long I knew she was watching me again, but I kept on reading until she spoke.

"All right, so I'm not free," she said, wistfully, reopening our conversation. "If you know so much, how would you diagnose my problem?"

"Put the Tarot cards away and I'll tell you."

"*Why* are you so demanding of your way?" she said angrily, slamming the cards together in her hand.

"Because I don't play games," I told her, closing my Bible and looking over at her. "If you want to talk with me you'll have to put away the devil's toys."

Much to my surprise, she opened her bag and shoved the Tarot cards inside.

"Okay, go ahead. Tell me." She folded her arms on her chest and shot her chin out.

"It's not going to be pretty and probably different from what you've heard before. Still want to hear it?"

"Yup. Shoot."

"Okay. When you were smaller you made more of your own decisions, but lately you've been *driven* to do things. A strange force inside you pulls you into experiences and relationships. Your whole life is a maze of rebellion as you buck one standard after another. Yet you think you'll find a solution in overthrowing this present system and joining others like yourself. You hate government in any form, but you know deep inside your life won't be worth much if real anarchy comes. Chaos reigns in a myopic universe where each person sits on a personal throne, living for self. Others who think the way you do would just as soon kill you as wink at you in a fight over one piece of bread.

"Your disease, in a word, is *rebellion*—a clenched fist jabbed toward God, His Word, and His Son. Your ultimate rejection of Him, even as your Creator, is expressed by your rebellion against your role as a woman . . ."

It was too much. For the first time Debbie's eyes got misty. Soon tears trickled down her face as she turned away from me and looked out the window.

"I never thought of it that way. I used to think that being a woman was the greatest."

"It can be," I said softly, looking away from her and sitting back in my seat again, "but only as a daughter of the King."

"What do you mean by that?"

"You've got to become a member of God's family, His royal family. And the only way that can happen is to be born into it—born from above, by faith in Jesus Christ. He died for you, shed His blood for you, because He loves you. It's not His will that you be bound by anything that *has you.* He wants to set you free to love Him and people for His sake. If you'll come to Him, admitting you are powerless to change yourself, He'll make you a new person."

Her eyes narrowed to mean little slits.

"I've heard that before and I don't buy it," she said.

I shrugged my shoulders.

"Then you'll just have to stay in those invisible chains until you're ready to come to Him on His terms. He didn't die to save you *in* your sin; only *from* your sin."

"I'm not ready for anything like that," she admitted, with sudden candor. "But I do thank you for talking to me. It's been well, different. And I do believe you're real. I mean, you don't come across as a hypocrite."

We both sat quietly for a minute. I prayed silently, pondering over what to do next. Finally, I turned in my seat to face her again.

"I appreciate your honesty, Debbie," I said. "There's a *time* to be born into the family of God, and He's the only one who knows exactly when a baby is ready to be born. I'll pray He'll bring you to that place of readiness. If I send you a Bible, will you read it?"

"No, I probably won't," she said frankly.

"Then I won't send you one. Let me see what I do have with me."

I foraged through the mini-jungle of my pocketbook. All I could find was a tract I had written on "The Exorcist or the Deliverer." I pulled it out and handed it to her.

"You wrote this, Pat?" she asked, surprised.

"Yes. That's 'my thing.' "

"Well, I *will* read this. And I'll think about what you said. Who knows, maybe some day I'll get desperate."

"Oh, you will, all right. With what you've got inside you, life will get more and more complicated and less and less pleasant. One day you will *long* to be set free."

"Can I have your address in case I ever want to contact you?" she asked suddenly. "I mean, if what you say is true, there may not be anyone around who understands when I'm ready to fly apart!"

"Sure," I said, taking the tract back again so that I could put my name and address on the back of it. "But whether you can reach me or not, you can always reach the Lord Jesus Christ. All you have to do is call on Him with all your heart, and you will find Him. He is God's Son, risen from the dead, and He will hear you. He is always *there,* in life's most desperate moments. As a Bible teacher I heard once said, 'He only waits to be wanted.' "

She took the tract and began to read. Before she had finished the first paragraph she began to nod. Soon she was fast asleep. I reached over and put the tract in her pocketbook.

"Lord, don't let her sleep into eternity like that," I whispered. "Wake her up before it's too late."

I went back to my reading and was deeply engrossed by the time the voice of the stewardess came over the speaker.

"Fasten your seat belts, ladies and gentlemen. Please observe the no-smoking sign. We are now starting our descent toward the Albany County Airport, serving Albany, Schenectady, and Troy."

Debbie woke up and clutched the arms of her seat. As I glanced over I saw fear of death written all over her blanched, taut face. It belied her bravado; made a mockery of her attempt to justify her life; betrayed her in her claim to have found life's answers.

I put my hand over on her arm and smiled at her as she looked across the seat that separated us, startled.

"God's got the whole world in His hands, Debbie," I said, softly, "including you and me. One of these days you're going to know Him and love Him for who He is. He made you for Himself and He's not going to give up His search to bring you all the way to Him. A poet once called God 'the hound of heaven.' "

The wheels hit the pavement and we bounced just a little as the pilot brought our plane to a quick stop.

"Thanks for caring about me," Debbie blurted out, as I stood to reach for both of our jackets on the overhead rack. "I'll never forget this trip and the talk we had."

"I'll be praying for you, Debbie. Have a good time with your father, and God bless you," I said, as I turned to leave.

Dick, my husband, was walking up the hall as I came

through the gate. His face lit up when he saw me, and he reached me with several big strides, giving me a quick hug. It's good to be welcomed back home, when you've been away.

Some day there's going to be a great reunion, when we all get Home. Every member of the family will be welcomed and have some praise from the Father, for His Word says so. And on that day I expect to see Debbie, transformed and radiant. Shackles gone forever then, I trust she'll be there with a multitude who have found Jesus as Lord. Only He can bring her to that point of surrender and faith. Only He can wipe away every tear and heal every ache left by the present boss of her life, the old deceiver himself.

As Dick and I walked to our car, I told him about Debbie. We rode along in silence for a few minutes.

"A penny for your thoughts," Dick finally said.

"I'm thinking of a vivid memory of another conversation about the woman's role I had once when your boss in California took us on his cabin cruiser, just a few months before he died. Remember that day?"

"Sure do. But not much of the talk. It was rough and I had to help him bring the cruiser in. Why, that was almost twenty years ago, Pat!"

"But it seems like yesterday, now," I mused.

3 *Finding Our Feminine Role*

Basking in the afternoon sunshine a mile or two beyond the Golden Gate Bridge, we women had a lively discussion. Dick and I and one other couple were guests of Dick and Jeanette Fayram on their cabin cruiser. The men were up forward, as they turned the boat and prepared to bring her in; the girls were sitting in the cockpit talking.

Suddenly a remark from one of the women rocked me more than the deepening swells underneath us.

"My Dad is a psychiatrist," she said. "He thinks women should be educated and trained for what they are really going to *do*. In other words, if they think they want to be homemakers, they should major in Home Ec in college and look on that as their creative outlet. Then they won't find life at home a stifling, mundane *bore*!"

"You mean he thinks we're being trained to be frustrated?" I asked, slowly turning this revolutionary thought over in my mind.

"Exactly," she answered. "We are brought up in a culture with a two-faced equality for women, offering education in any field open to a man. Then we marry him and find out he doesn't want us competing with him at all."

"Perhaps it's because family needs haven't changed much over the ages," Jeanette said. "Married life brings certain responsibilities that have to be carried out. Maybe most modern men are willing to see their *daughters* grow up with the same advantages as their sons, but if their wives don't run things at home, who will? The days of household help are just about over, except for the very well-to-do. Especially on a full-time basis."

"That's true," I said. "Still, I don't know how these facts give you any more love for housework. Somehow I cannot picture myself being a Home Ec major back in college. My attitude was such that I'd have wanted to be an English major, anyway."

"I'm with you," the psychiatrist's daughter said. "But Dad thinks we are setting ourselves up for misery unless we change. He says we'll flip unless we adjust to the actual demands upon us, most of our lives."

"I don't know about that," I said, beginning to feel conviction. "After all, everyone is different. One woman may be *creative* making pies; another may find it a drag. Lots of us live more in the mind, don't you think?"

"Oh, I agree," she said, grabbing onto the rail as the boat lurched. "But Dad thinks we should also learn to work with our hands as well as our heads. You *can* train yourself to think while you cook or sew."

"Well, I'm glad I've been able to take a few courses in graduate school this year," I said, "and get involved where I can in civic affairs. The four walls close me in."

"Especially when the children are small in the winter," Jeanette said. "The flu follows the measles, and tonsillitis comes after the flu."

"Well, I've not had that yet," I said, "but even just the company of a toddler is far from stimulating. This last winter I'd have lost my mind if it weren't for the library and books, and later, the courses at Berkeley."

"My Dad would say that's all training, or lack of it," the first girl shouted over at me. By now the wind was blowing so hard and the engine revved up so much that real conversation was impossible.

Just ahead of us seemed to be a wall of water. I was glad Dick was in the cabin helping our host bring the boat in. He had lots of experience in this field, and it was an eloquent example of the difference between the sexes. I don't think any of us women wanted to compete in seamanship while a storm was brewing.

"But what does your Dad think is the *answer* to our predicament now that we're *here*?" I yelled across the cockpit.

"Oh, just hang on. They'll get us back somehow," she said, obviously having missed part of what I said. Suddenly she grabbed the rail, leaned overboard, and lost her share of our picnic lunch.

Now, nearly two decades later, that brief talk is as real to me as the storm which came up on the way home. The psychiatrist's daughter, whose name I have forgotten, helped me to realize *many* women feel trapped at home and have to come to grips with their role. Up to that point I had been fighting the battle of the mask: attempting to appear happy in a confinement that often stifled me.

I did not know then the value of complete honesty with myself and with God. I could have learned something from a four-year-old, who vented his emotions aloud one day in the bathtub.

As his mother walked by the bathroom door, she heard sounds of splashing and a sing-song refrain from her son. Fascinated, she stopped to listen.

"I will not take a bath or change my clothes, I will not eat spinach or make wee-wee for them. I will not brush my hair or clean my room. I will chop their heads off and stuff them in the garbage can.

"I will eat candy bars and ice cream for breakfast. I will not wear any sox. I will never hear them when they call me. I will play in mud all day and leave my tracks on all the rugs. I will chop their heads off and stuff them in the garbage can."

What that mother heard was a child taking off his "good boy" mask and getting down to bare skin. The burden of trying to say what he ought rather than what he thought had simply proved too much for a four-year-old mind.

Sooner or later most of us get tired of play-acting. A friend recently told me, "I smiled and lied my way through life until I met Christ. Now my smile is spontaneous or I don't bother. I tell the truth even though it hurts."

Society teaches us to put on appropriate masks for every situation of life. Often the successful person is a most skillful mask-adjuster. He sizes up situations and people and fits himself to them. If someone is good at this business, we tend to think of him as *tactful, mature;* if he is not convincing, we call him *two-faced.*

It is a great relief to discover that God ignores masks and sees the real person beneath. Therefore it is useless to wear one with Him. The Lord Jesus Christ reserved His firmest warnings for hypocrites. In fact, He told many other kinds of sinners they would have "a place with the hypocrites," implying they are first in line for hell!

In ancient Greek drama the word *hupocrites* meant a mask worn by actors in the open air amphitheater. Since the audience sat on a hill above the flat, open stage area, masks had to be large enough for a device inside to amplify the voice. Features on the mask were exaggerated, caricatured, so that the part or role being played might be quickly identified. Often a few actors had to play many parts. Thus a change of mask gave the audience its only clue to new identities.

Over the centuries between the Golden Age of Pericles to the first century, A.D., the word *hupocrites* came to mean the mask-wearer rather than the mask. The only person who used this word in the New Testament was Jesus Christ, but He used it many times. His warnings to hypocrites are relevant today, and His cure for the mask-wearer is still the same.

We often call a person a hypocrite if he knows his faults and tries to hide them carefully in order to fool others. Yet such a person does not necessarily have a big problem with deception. He may be honest in his self-evaluation and desperate in his attempts to please those who matter to him. Yet, like the little boy in the bathtub, he cannot take off his mask until he is alone. He feels truth is too risky.

The true hypocrite is the one who is self-deceived and unaware of his state. He honestly believes himself to be the person his mask conveys. His whole life is a gigantic deception, not just in his relationship with others, but in his attitude toward God and himself. How wretched we are in that state! Like blind moles in the daylight, we are ignorant of the beauty of earth bathed in daylight because we have never seen it.

I once knew a woman who was a classic example of this type of hypocrisy. She believed herself to be a woman of God, hearing frequently from Him. She went to the right meetings, sang the right songs, knew the right people. She read her Bible rather frequently and knew a few verses by heart. Others admired her for her stand.

Then slowly her life began to grow sour. She took a wrong turn in her thinking, and could not seem to get back off the bypass. Several who knew her well said all that happened was that she became jealous of the spiritual gifts of others.

Unfortunately, that was enough. Evidently she set the rudder of her human will on a course directly opposed to God's revealed will in the Bible. Jealousy is never His will. The apostle James wrote, "But if you have bitter jealousy and selfish ambition in your heart, do not be arrogant and so lie against the truth. This wisdom is not that which comes down from above, but is earthly, natural, demonic. For where jealousy and selfish ambition exist, there is disorder and every evil thing" (James 3:14-16).

With willful sin came the inevitable result: deception. Like Eve, who believed the serpent's lie rather than God's Word, this woman's life began to show forth very poor fruit.

First came false guidance and a strange arrogance in defending her position; next came loss of interest in spiritual things on the part of others in her family, including open rebellion and behavior problems with one child. Finally this poor woman became a victim of compulsive patterns of action.

There is no way out of such a maze other than to return to the place where we entered it and repent.

When God met me I was a compulsive do-gooder. I believed the respectable, cheerful mask I wore was the real me. However, beneath my civic accomplishments and "churchianity" there was a seething unrest. I was caught in a maze of hostility I could neither explain nor escape. I feared nothing so much as a kind of mental dry rot which would atrophy my dreams and crush my intellect, in those days of the boat-trip conversation.

One day the Lord Jesus brought me to the end of myself and poured His life into my parched spirit. The whole story is told in my book, *Out! In the Name of Jesus* (Creation House). Suffice it to say here that confrontation with Him made me able to confront myself, take off my mask, and find out what it means to be a daughter of the King. Boredom gave way to glad adventure. Now, having a relationship of love with the most wonderful Person there is, I found myself wanting to please Him. He quenched every thirst I had.

Thirsty women are nothing new. Jesus encountered one on a trip through Samaria. Sitting near a well at noon time, He asked a woman who had come there, "Give me a drink" (John 4:7).

She was surprised that He stooped to speak to her, for He was a Jew. She knew Jews usually looked down on her people. Besides that, she was a woman! It is hard for us in the western world to appreciate how much the Gospel has affected our feminine stature. Everywhere Christ is preached, His standard for women follows. "In Christ there is no male or female" (Galatians 3:28), but in the unredeemed world it is far different. There are many places yet where a cow brings a better price than a bride!

How startled this daughter of Eve must have been when she heard Jesus' full offer (John 4:10-16):

> "If you knew the gift of God, and who it is who says to you, 'Give Me a drink,' you would have asked Him, and He would have given you living water."
>
> She said to Him, "Sir, you have nothing to draw with and the well is deep; where then do You get that living water? You are not greater than our father Jacob, are You, who gave us the well, and drank of it himself, and his sons, and his cattle?"
>
> Jesus answered and said to her, "Everyone who drinks of this water shall thirst again; but whoever drinks of the water that I shall give him shall never thirst; but the water that I shall give him shall become in him a well of water springing up to eternal life."
>
> The woman said to Him, "Sir, give me this water, so I will not be thirsty, nor come all the way here to draw."
>
> He said to her, "Go call your husband, and come here."

Now, this woman believed in the "new morality." How perplexed she must have been when she heard that question. Should she keep on a mask, and pretend she was married? Or could she risk telling the truth to this wonderful Stranger?

Her thirst won out.

"I have no husband," she admitted (John 4:17a).

She soon found out she had made the right choice. He already knew all about her, anyway.

"You have well said, 'I have no husband,' for you have had five husbands and the one whom you have now is not your husband; this you have said truly" (John 4:17a-18).

That hurt. The conversation was getting too personal. So she changed the subject—from her lifestyle, to religious observance. (Don't we do the same?)

But she underestimated Him. He always knows how to get our attention again! Hear Him draw her, and us, back to the real matter of importance:

> "But an hour is coming, and now is, when the true worshipers shall worship the Father in spirit and in truth; for such people the Father seeks to be His worshipers. God is spirit; and those who worship Him must worship in spirit and truth."
>
> The woman said to Him, "I know that Messiah is coming (He who is called Christ); when that One comes, He will declare all things to us."
>
> Jesus said to her, "I who speak to you am He."

She allowed Him to show her who she really was. This stripping of her mask prepared her to receive a revelation of who *He* really is.

Can it be any different for you or for me?

In those early days in California, just months after the boat trip, I found the Lord Jesus was my peace, my joy. His living water gave me a new will to try to work on a faltering marriage, and find out what mothering was supposed to be all about.

I began searching the Scriptures, for the first time in my life. I almost dreaded what I might find there, with regard to the female role. Somehow I had a vague notion, which I had carried around for years, that God wanted women held down.

What a surprise I had when I found Proverbs 31. Why, an excellent wife is *not* an unbearable bore, after all! The specter of a drudge imprisoned in her kitchen vanished for good once I discovered God's "pattern" woman. No mealy-mouthed Pollyanna, she is a sparkling individual with an immense variety of interests and creative activities. She is not a servile mimic of her husband's ideas, either. Her great strength lies in the unique dignity, wisdom, and kindness which the Lord gives His daughters who fear and love Him.

The emancipated, redeemed woman of Proverbs 31 is no hysterical shrew waving banners and shrieking obscenities. The freedom God gives His feminine servants does not come by demanding. It is inherent in the life He gives when He gives Himself. "Strength and dignity are her *clothing,*" not her clutched spoil; she wears them with a perfect fit.

God's pattern woman has respect and praise from her family and the community because of *what she is. What she does* is a natural outworking of the creative, divine life at work within her.

The notable gal of Proverbs 31 is an essential vice-president in the family corporation, not a closet executive brought out for rare occasions. She is a producer, not a parasite, in the family economy. Yet she comes across in no stereotype of our own time. She is neither "just a housewife" nor a working mother. She is a partner in the family team. She sees what needs doing and does it.

Perhaps the key sentence of that whole section is, "Her husband is known in the gates." Is God saying that masculine fulfillment and stature are directly related to the quality of support and service his wife gives?

Years later I got into even more basic Scriptures, Genesis 2 and 3. How did it all start, anyway? What did God specifically have in mind when He made *woman*?

Here I found some real shockers. (Perhaps I couldn't have stood them in the earlier years.)

> Then the Lord God said, "It is not good for the man to be alone; I will make him a helper suitable for him!" . . .
>
> So the Lord God caused a deep sleep to fall upon the man, and he slept; then He took one of his ribs, and closed up the flesh at that place. And the Lord God fashioned into a woman the rib which He had taken from the man, and brought her to the man. And the man said, "This is now bone of my bones, and flesh of my flesh; and shall be called woman because she was taken out of the man."
>
> For this cause a man shall leave his father and his mother, and shall cleave to his wife; and they shall become one flesh. (Genesis 2:18; 21-24.)

So, we women were *not* created to be independent, *competing* with men. We were meant to complement or *complete* them. What a difference from my early attitudes! No wonder they never worked. Can you imagine a spoon being manufactured which would try to be used as a knife? Instead of supporting and helping, always cutting and chopping to pieces! It's a miracle the Creator did not throw me away, the way a manufacturer would have, if the thing he made did not perform as it was designed to do.

But God is loving and merciful and—bless Him—long-suffering. He sometimes waits a long time before we *see* something with the eyes of faith. It has just been the last few years that I have finally *seen* what God wants of His daughters. Redeemed femininity has a high calling. No matter who hurts, we are always to *help*; nothing less is worthy of our created role.

We come from a side of man that he can never get back except in feminine form. He aches without it; we yearn to be that complementary complex of attributes and are happy when we are.

God has a way for us that works, every time. When we walk in it the path grows brighter step by step. The climate in our homes can change from cloudy and rainy to *sunny,* most of the time. Perhaps a simple acrostic will help us to remember His way:

W   for *winsomeness;* an old-fashioned word Webster defines as "delightful; attractive in *appearance, character* and *manner."* (That covers everything, doesn't it? Body, soul, and spirit!)

A   for *acceptance* of others, just the way they are. How important this is in our attitude toward God, to accept Him as He is and His Word as it is! Then we look for the *changes in ourselves,* not in the people He uses as sandpaper to make us His "polished shaft."

Y   for *yieldedness* to Jesus as Lord, or absolute authority in our lives. Then we can submit with ease to earthly authority "as unto the Lord," for this qualifying phrase nullifies every unrighteous demand upon us. *We yield only to His will in every situation, every relationship of life.*

What freedom is this way! Not license to do as we please—but *liberty, to do as He pleases!* He *is* the Way; His Word sheds light on every step; His Spirit empowers us to put our footsteps firmly where He has gone before.

Thanks to Him, I can shout from my innermost heart, "I'm glad I'm a woman!" (I hated it, before.) Now I get up each new morning hardly able to wait for the challenge each day holds for me as a daughter of the King!

But not all see it that way, yet. One day I got a phone call that started like this:

"Pat, I'm desperate. I've had it with this marriage. Either I'm going to have to do something drastic soon, or I will go stark, raving mad! Every time that idiot I'm married to walks in the door I feel like throwing up. I was on my way to the garage to turn on the engine, but I thought I'd call you first. Somehow I decided to ask you if I should go through with that . . ."

4 *The Women's Retreats Are Born*

"Ladies, how can we meet the needs of women who are desperate?" I asked my Bible study soon after that phone call. "What can we do to provide a way where they can share ideas with others and find out if they have spiritual needs which can be met through the ministries in the Holy Spirit?"

"You mean people who want to kill themselves, things like that?"

"Yes. Things like that. The whole problem is that Bible studies are often avoided by those who need them most. People who are wrapped up in personal problems are seldom disciplined enough to get into the regular, systematic study of the Word."

"There ought to be a way to make them thirsty," one girl bubbled. "After all, doesn't the Bible say we are *salt?* What does salt do but make you thirsty?"

"I always thought that meant we were to be the *preservative* of the earth," a quieter girl said, directing her comment to the vivacious woman who had just spoken.

"Well, salt makes things *tasty,* too," another offered, cheerfully. "I sure don't like food without it, and I don't think the Lord likes a drab, boring church, either. I think our salt is that special zest He gives us that the world doesn't have. Joy, sparkle, bounce—the whole bit."

"That'll make them thirsty, all right!"

"But *how* can we share it with those who need it so much?" I broke in.

"Do you think we could plan a retreat that was, say, not terribly *religious?* We could do plenty of praying ahead of time, but keep the actual meetings more like a sharing time. What I'm suggesting is an opportunity for various ones to speak on areas in which they have victory, followed by buzz groups where we would divide the women who come for discussion periods."

"You mean teaching followed by discussion, rather than the usual singing, prayer, and talking, with no opportunity to share?"

"Right. We don't want to turn off those not ready to praise the Lord. We want to *reach* them. Then they'll *have* something to praise the Lord about later."

"I think it will work, if we give the women a chance to share among themselves," an older friend commented, who had been quiet so far. "Women need a chance to talk things over. That's what's wrong with the big conference approach."

"Then we'll need discussion leaders, so the sharing times will accomplish something and not go too far afield," another chimed in.

"I'll bet one of the biggest heartaches women face is where their husbands are not fully committed to the Lord," Kay said. She is a polio victim who has worn braces and been on crutches for many years; yet none of us had ever heard her express pity for herself.

"You could teach them how to walk that road, Kay," I said. Immediately there were vigorous nods of agreement, all around the room. "How about a message on 'The Unequal Yoke'?"

Kay looked surprised but smiled.

"I'd really have to trust the Lord, but if it would help anybody else, I'd be glad to do it."

"Someone ought to share how God got the victory in the lives of their rebellious teenagers," another girl said.

"And what a joy it is when years of prayers are answered," Eleanore said. "My oldest daughter has just come back to the Lord after almost fifteen years away."

"Everyone ought to hear that story," someone broke in.

"Right! Who better than Eleanore could tell it, whose kids are all grown now, and every one of them walking with the Lord!"

It went on like that for an hour longer. We were amazed that before the group broke up we had four speakers, several discussion leaders for small groups, and even a coordinator for the whole project. Fran Kraus, a pastor's wife, was ideal for that job. With her six children she had a ready labor force to make name tags for us, too.

We decided to have the tags in several colors, and assign women into groups by color. That way we could give each woman in a group a different color as she walked in. This would tend to break up cliques. I had taken a graduate course in group dynamics and remembered learning that people often shared more easily with strangers.

Soon afterward we signed up for a community room in a local bank for two days in May. We publicized the retreat, or conference, only by word of mouth, and wondered what would happen.

The weeks of planning sped by, and we found ourselves with an expectant, bubbly group that sparkling spring morning the retreat began. Grandmothers and brides were there, as well as a group of women with teenagers at home. Protestants, Catholics, and unchurched women came.

It was a simple format. Each speaker taught for an hour; then the buzz groups would discuss questions she provided to the leaders, for the next hour. We had four rounds like this over a two-day period.

The secret of the Lord's blessing on the meetings lay in the fact that we were solidly in His will. Today some believe that the apostle Paul would not allow a woman to teach. Yet he wrote a letter to Titus, urging that they do so.

> 'Older women likewise are to be reverent in their behavior, not malicious gossips, nor enslaved to much wine, teaching what is good, that they may encourage the young women to love their husbands, to love their children, to be sensible, pure, workers at home, being subject to their own husbands, that the Word of God may not be dishonored.' (Titus 2:3-5.)

The genius of the idea, even with those who did not know the Lord or care about His will, was the fact that the subject matter was really "where it was at." Few that came had not faced some kind of family problem at one time or another. Some women commented that never, in Sunday School or catechism classes, had they had an opportunity like this one to be taught on the pitfalls and good approaches of family situations or to discuss them so frankly.

Erline Valentine, a dynamic young black woman, went home determined to put into practice the things she had learned. Although she was a Bible study teacher herself, she gained some new insights on her role as a wife. She began praising her husband that night, rather than "reminding" him of his failures. He responded by telling her to go to more of those retreats, no matter what else had to be dropped!

One girl complained that she had been dragged to the meetings on false pretenses by a neighbor. Then, in the kind of paradox common to our sex she added, "But I wouldn't have missed this for the world."

The talks on marital roles stressed the importance of communication, sex, submission to the husband (except if he required a wife to sin), and *changing one's attitude* to one of willingness to accommodate.

Glowing with the love of Christ, Kay tactfully presented as *opportunities* those occasions in the home when her Christian testimony brought criticism and restrictions upon her. She mentioned her husband's preference for her to attend pinochle parties with him on Saturday nights. She tried to be available to those who might be spiritually hungry and ask her questions during such evenings.

Kay also shared her calm submission to the "no church" regulation whenever her husband requested it of her. For a while he took the whole family snowmobiling on Sundays. She emphasized how the Lord worked the situation out, as she prayed. When the novelty wore off, she and her children were free to go back to church!

In the question period before the buzz groups met, Kay was asked how to answer a husband who wanted to take his wife into a bar. Without a second's hesitation, she said, "Go ahead *in faith* and let your light shine there. I guarantee if you use the opportunity there for Jesus, witnessing to people and passing out tracts, he won't ask you to go back!"

Before the conference was over, one woman stood up and said Kay's radiance and victory as she shared her difficult experiences meant more to her than anything else from the two days. She realized that Kay was a living testimony to the fact that God's grace *is* sufficient for the hardest trials life has to offer. With the Lord Jesus, no one should go down in defeat.

Friday morning Eleanore Smith spoke on the mother's role. The women listened spellbound as she told it "like it was"—how God had dealt with Carl and her before He brought back two of their children to Himself. She stressed the remarkable change in her own life and attitude because of deliverance from demonic oppression, and her baptism in the Holy Spirit.

Finally, Eleanore shared how God had taught them to *praise Him* for their indifferent daughter, even in her rebellion.

"We read Merlin Carothers' book, *Prison to Praise,* and applied its message of praise in all circumstances," she said. "Two weeks later our daughter Gincie came back to the Lord in a beautiful way."

A special highlight afterward was Gincie's own testimony, giving powerful credibility to all that Eleanore had said. Admitting that she had been "something of an authority on rebellious teenagers," Gincie said that she had been powerless to change through those early years. She also testified to the mighty change in her life when the Lord delivered her from invisible bonds.

Gincie showed the power of the Lord Jesus in many ways in her life—His meeting their needs in times of tight finances, and healing their children instantly on several occasions since she had come into the life in the Spirit. She closed with the wonderful news of her husband's conversion just a few weeks previously. This was a special encouragement to a number of girls present who were praying to that end in their own households.

Last I spoke on the woman as a "daughter of the King." The Spirit of God impressed upon me the need for each woman to realize that her relationship with the Lord is one that is neither marred nor made by earthly cricumstances. Anyone can excel here, because the Lord Jesus is perfect. Yielding to Him—dwelling and abiding in His presence—brings great joy to the life whether the earthly marriage is happy or not.

The thoughts of that simple message have been shared with thousands since. My convictions have deepened about them as I have seen many lives of God's feminine servants molded by Him into daughters of the King.

We can only become a princess in the royal family by being born into it. The new birth, like the earthly one, is initiated by an act of the Father. His seed is the Word of God which becomes lodged in our hearts. Under the nurture of the Holy Spirit, that Word brings conviction of sin and stirrings begin which lead to the crisis experience of conversion: being "born again."

Only God knows when a baby is ready to be born. Doctors, nurses, or midwives may help when the time is right, but they dare not tamper with the onset of labor. Other people around the person needing Christ may help to point that one to the Savior and bring him or her to a place of decision. But the moment of new birth is a divinely ordained one, just like physical birth.

Once in the royal family, the King's daughter finds she has a very different life from her common one, of this world. Now she is preparing for a wedding with the heavenly Bridegroom! Since "The King's daughter is all glorious within" (Psalm 45:13), she must lay great stress on inner adornment. Victory in the thought life is won by a steady diet of Scripture daily, to feed the spirit. She must read in a regular pattern (see *Out! in the Name of Jesus* or *Using Your Spiritual Authority* for the system I use) and meditate upon it, seeking to apply it to all of her life. I memorize one verse of Scripture daily as a kind of spiritual "vitamin pill." Our children memorize systematically under the program of the Bible Memory Association.

Not only is Scripture our *food,* however. It is also our *weaponry.* In the spiritual warfare which all of the King's family are engaged in, showing forth His light in this dark world, we also need memorized Scripture in close conflict with the powers of darkness. Both of my books mentioned above have the same appendix containing verses we recommend for this purpose. They are listed under headings which represent major areas of failure in human life. These attitudes also have demonic spirits named in the same way. When these are oppressing a life, they can make defeat almost inevitable. Thus the Bible verses listed serve both functions mentioned here. When memorized, they are *food* for the new life, born of the Spirit of God; they are also *weaponry* against the evil spirits connected with wrong attitudes.

Spiritual warfare is a subject which should be taught thoroughly or not at all. It is an area in which a *little* knowledge can be dangerous if wrongly applied. Therefore if you wish to know more I urge you to read the books mentioned. Suffice it to say here that if you have habits which control *you;* have headaches, dizziness, or nausea; get sleepy praying or reading the Word; are restless or very talkative; have mental or emotional problems, you may need to do this reading and seek deliverance. If you have ever dabbled in the occult, you are almost certainly in need.

The King's daughters should live radiantly beyond the power of any defeat, for the King has won a full victory over all His enemies! Calvary brought the death wound to the old serpent's head. The problem with the church has been that the wily devil and his crew have attempted to keep us from finding that out.

When the Lord Jesus Christ called His twelve disciples, He did so for three purposes: "that they might be with Him, and that He might send them out to preach, and to have authority to cast out the demons" (Mark 3:14,15). By and large His present-day disciples obey only two of these commands. Thus they reap the results of souring fruit and tormented believers. *When the preaching of the Gospel is not accompanied by the casting out of evil spirits, people often bring their problems into the church with them.* Praise our wonderful Lord that He is remedying that situation today and raising up obedient servants who follow His standards rather than their own prejudices.

In addition to having the Scripture as food and weaponry, giving victory over evil in her life, the true daughter of the King has a thankful and merry heart. She must learn the value of singing her way through life, both literally and figuratively. Then she finds that praise silences the whine of complaint with the whisper of love.

It was thrilling to see some women born into the King's family during the two days of that first retreat. One desperate girl admitted that she had planned to commit suicide just before the phone rang, bringing an invitation to the conference from a complete stranger. Not only did she come to Christ, but she also went home and complimented her husband for the first time in a decade of marriage!

Others came to the Lord in the weeks following, as a direct result of the retreat. One, a college professor's wife I invited, was touched by the atmosphere in the meetings. A year later when she visited this area again after moving away, she asked the Lord to come into her life.

One delegate brought a lifetime friend to whom she had witnessed for years without success. The Holy Spirit melted this girl's heart through the simplicity and warmth of the speakers and those in her discussion group. She came to the Lord a few days later.

We all knew we had only begun to see what God would do through such times. As I helped Fran Kraus out with the few books left that Friday afternoon, she voiced what many of us felt.

"You know, I have the feeling we have just tossed a pebble into a great pond, leaving ripples which will continue to spread out in wider and wider circles until Jesus gets back!"

She was a good prophet. By fall of 1972 we were having similar interdenominational retreats one day a month at Pineview Community Church in Albany. Several outstanding Bible teachers spoke, as well as a number of "unknowns" with testimonies to share. The "pebbles" began to cause wider and wider circles of influence. Requests for speaking engagements which came to me were often for pilot retreats of a similar type in other cities. This trend has developed to such an extent that I now speak three times on the woman's role for every once on spiritual warfare. When one considers that my first two books were on the subject of the latter, this fact is remarkable indeed. In other words, the crying need of women across the country today seems to be in finding their Godly feminine role. All other matters are secondary.

A particularly dramatic result from one of those early

retreats was an instance of a Catholic girl leading a new girl to the Lord, right in a buzz group. So ecstatic was she over this new experience of soul-winning that she went home and led her husband to Christ in the same way, that night!

I wrote an article on the retreats for *Christian Life* magazine entitled, "You Can Learn To Love." In it the Rev. Gordon Kraus was mentioned, who had master tapes of all the messages. He had two dozen requests for tapes within a month, from all over the country. A year later when I spoke in Dallas a woman came to me thanking me for that early message on "A Daughter of the King," assuring me they were holding retreats in her area. Letters I received that year also indicated a number of other groups were trying the simple format with much the same blessing.

After two years our local retreats bogged down, however, primarily from lack of organization and proper leadership on a continuing basis. About that time I won a writers' contest sponsored by Logos, and was sent to their Writers' Workshop. There I met Katie Fortune, editor of *Algow Magazine,* and heard for the first time about the Women's Aglow Fellowship. Katie promised to send me more information, and by the summer of 1974 Aglow was organized with excellent leadership here in the Albany-Troy-Schenectady-Saratoga area.

Now Aglow holds retreats several times a year, interspersed with banquets and other programs. It is a healthy balance, and we are reaching a wider segment of women than ever before in the Capital District.

Why not try it in your area?

Please don't get the idea you will "live happily ever after" if you do, however. The devil hates the kind of mask-stripping honesty such retreats have, and especially the changes in lives for the better which inevitably follow.

I was to get some of my hardest blows in the school of hard knocks just after this program was successfully launched. It all began when my husband was in Florida, attending the fiftieth wedding anniversary of his parents.

5 *Encountering God's "Hornets"*

That whole September weekend in 1972 was a nightmare. Dick had flown southward for the golden wedding festivities just hours before I came down with a miserable infection. Head, neck, back, thighs and calves—everything ached. The fever persisted for days. It felt to me like my old enemy from missionary days, malaria.

The children were marvelous through it all. They did all the cooking and ran up and down stairs for me dozens of times. They cleaned up the living and family rooms for the New Testament Fellowship that met in our home in those days.

On Sunday I listened to the singing and worship for the first time from my bed. I sent word down to the elders that I would like to have them pray for me and anoint me with oil before they left.

They came upstairs, good friends we had been meeting with since the fall of 1970. I tried to sit up as they gathered around my bed to pray, but I couldn't make it. They passed the oil quietly from one to another, and each one daubed a little on his finger. Then they laid hands on me, prayed, and left.

We had seen dozens of people healed in this way. After all, God's Word says, "Is anyone among you sick? Let him call for the elders of the church, and let them pray over him, anointing him with oil in the name of the Lord; and the prayer offered in faith will restore the one who is sick, and the Lord will raise him up, and if he has committed sins, they will be forgiven him" (James 5:14, 15).

There were lots of cheery calls up the stairs before the group left.

"You'll be well in no time."

"Might as well get up and start hopping around now,

because you're already healed."

"When Dick gets back, he won't even know you've been sick!"

" 'Bye, Pat. Let us know if there is anything we can do."

Before long they were all gone, and it was quiet again. But I did not get better. In fact, the next day I was much worse.

Monday afternoon I was rushed to Saratoga Hospital. It was awkward in the emergency room, for we had no family doctor. There was no room available, but the admitting physician said I was too ill to be sent home. He located an empty bed for me somewhere, and I spent the night in an upper hall a few yards away from an elderly woman who groaned her way through the night.

The pain in my head and chest became so severe that I asked for medication. A nurse brought me aspirin with codeine, and I lay there, praying and wondering whether the children would get off to school on time in the morning. Actually, I knew they would. Charlie and Johnny were both still home then, a senior and junior in high school. Friends in the Fellowship had brought them up to see me in the emergency room after they got home from school. Others had taken Beth Ann and Billy through supper time. It was a long, bewildering night. Dozens of questions crowded into my mind.

The next day doctors found no malarial parasites and assumed I had been hit with a bad dose of the flu. I was put in the cardiac wing and ordered complete bed rest.

Within a few days I began to feel better; a week later I was home. What a blow it was to find out that I was not really *well*. My strength simply would not return, and I found myself spending twenty-one of the twenty-four hours of each day in bed. I dragged myself downstairs to get the children off to school at breakfast and somehow stumbled through a similar ordeal at supper time. Dick was helpful, and insisted that I not overdo. But even after several weeks, I did not have my strength back.

Having the New Testament Fellowship meet in the house on Sundays became a real burden. I was not able to help the family in any way, and the entire responsibility fell on them. My husband and I finally asked the group to find another place to meet.

The elders decided to seek the will of God for our group. Did He want us to continue meeting on Sundays or go back into regular churches, keeping only the prayer meeting? Did He have another place for us?

A general meeting was held one evening for all members of the Fellowship. Many said the group had meant a great deal to them. One person said, "It's unthinkable that we'd break up, now. We should go on together. Let's find another place to meet."

When the vote came it was unanimous to continue. Dick and I voted with the others so as not to dissent from the will of the group. But we honestly wondered, "Is God saying, *stop*?"

Very soon afterward a Grange hall became available to us at a nominal rent, and we began to meet there on Sundays. The prayer meeting was moved from home to home on a monthly basis. Thus much of the burden for the Fellowship was no longer on our family.

Yet Dick and I still had questions. If we really *were* in the will of God in the pattern we were following, why was my health so slow in returning? Were we completely fair to our teenage boys, who were teaching the children and young people of our small group? Suppose they still needed fellowship with a larger group of their peers?

And what about Sunday nights? Was it fair to get together with a few couples from our same small group for Bible study, when the children were left home alone? Years of spiritual grounding in evangelical churches told us this was wrong. The pattern of informal worship for the whole family on Sunday nights was deeply ingrained in us. We began to realize how much we missed it.

In January, 1973, Dick made a decision which was to change the whole direction of our lives as a family. He took us to a Sunday evening service at Pineview Community Church in Albany, the church that was hosting the ladies' retreats. It so happens that Pineview is a Christian and Missionary Alliance Church, which was our own denomination. We felt more "at home" that night than at any time since our move up north from New Jersey.

From then on we attended Pineview on Sunday nights, and

noticed a happy improvement in every member of our family. Even my own health improved dramatically, and within a few weeks I could stay up all day, without even a nap.

Although the New Testament Fellowship limped along for another year and a half, other members began to follow the same pattern. They started drifting back into regular churches for Sunday nights and special meetings. Keeping the Sunday services going involved more and more effort; less and less joy. What was wrong? Was God trying to tell us something?

In October of 1973 the Fellowship had another general meeting, again to seek the Lord's will for the group. They voted unanimously to cancel Sunday services, keeping only the week night prayer meeting. I was away at the *Guideposts* Writer's Workshop that week. When I got home and heard the news, I felt great peace about the decision. Soon our family was totally involved in the program at Pineview. Most other Fellowship members became active members of churches as well.

It soon became apparent that God was using each family in its new church home. We had opportunities to share many of the things God had taught us in the smaller group, particularly concerning the deliverance ministry. When the New Testament Fellowship finally was disbanded in June of 1974, our prayer meeting became one of the regular neighborhood groups announced in the Pineview bulletin every week.

One day it hit me that getting us back into the churches was what God had been after, all along. I read Exodus 23 and was particularly struck by verses 20 and 28:

> "Behold, I am going to send an angel before you to guard you along the way, and to bring you into the place which I have prepared . . . And I will send *hornets* ahead of you, that they may drive out the Hivites, the Canaanites, and the Hittites before you."

I laughed right out loud as I thought of an old song I had heard missionaries sing, years ago in Nigeria. "When the people were not willing, God sent the hornets, and the hornets made them willing . . ." Something like that.

Too bad we had been so dull that God had to use the hornets on us, God's own people! Had my illness and other difficulties we experienced in the New Testament Fellowship been "hornets," driving us from comfortable ruts into fellowship with far more of the Body of Christ? The growth and opportunities for outreach we have experienced at Pineview convince me that this was so.

Looking out of my study window onto our winter landscape just now, I had another flash of insight. Much beauty and good solid earth is buried beneath that blanket of snow—*God's will for a time.* Snow in December is lovely, reasonable, and appropriate. But snow in July? Even the skiers around here don't expect that.

The Israelites of old moved when the cloud moved. They stayed in any spot only so long as God's presence (in the form of His Shekinah glory cloud) remained there. I see now that our small group was God's will for a time, but we were very slow to move on when it had served its purpose.

Today as I sit at my typewriter I am reminiscing on the past five years in which I and my family have been involved in the charismatic movement. I thank God for every experience, every relationship. He has taught me and my family a good deal. More than anything else, however, He has deepened our love and appreciation for His written Word, the Bible.

The Holy Spirit was given to the church so that His Word might become part of us and be lived out through us: not that we might bypass spiritual nourishment and discipline. He *empowers* us to love and feed on His Word as never before. Then we can act in accordance with *all of it,* not just favorite sections that agree with our theological prejudice.

Recently my good friend Eleanore Smith and I allowed ourselves the luxury of a long phone call discussing these things. (About once every month or two we catch up on the Lord's doings that we have both seen since the last chat.)

"You know, it's been just about five years since that meeting in March of 1970 when a number of us were baptized in the Spirit," I said.

"That's right," Eleanore agreed. "And a lot of water has gone under the bridge since."

"Look," I suggested. "You and I have stayed pretty much together in our thinking on these things, and I'll bet we have some of the same conclusions. What is the thing you're happiest or most relieved about, after five years?"

"That Carl had the good sense to insist we stay in our home church," she said, promptly. "I've watched a few of the 'come-outers' go completely down the drain, as far as a vital walk with the Lord is concerned."

"I can surely understand *that*," I said. "Small groups can teach a lot, but they are never going to replace the gospel lighthouse here in the United States."

"Are you sorry you ever got involved with the New Testament Fellowship, Pat?" she asked.

"No," I answered, slowly. "Some things have to be learned by going through them. Don't forget, we were getting helpful teaching in those early days."

"That's true," Eleanore said. "But some groups today seem to end up going off into heresy. Others are so legalistic they are festering with problems. I'm so glad our prayer group never tried to become a church. The whole purpose of our group is to disciple these young people so they will go back and work in their own churches as dynamic witnesses for the Lord Jesus Christ."

"Right!" I said. "And you've seen a lot of them go to the far corners of the earth with the Gospel, haven't you?"

"Yes," she replied. "Several have gone with YWAM (Youth with a Mission) to Germany, Switzerland, Holland, and even Korea. YWAM trains them in evangelism and encourages them to work with local churches wherever there are believing groups who will cooperate. Usually they enter an area at the invitation of a church."

"That sounds really good to me," I commented. "The thing that alarms me about this emphasis in some groups on 'submission' and 'eldership' is that *the elders within such a group submit only to each other*. They really do not see the need of testing ideas with other pastors and elders in their area. It *can* cause a vicious legalism that makes our problems in evangelical churches look mild, by comparison.

"Recently I was speaking in an area where the elders who

had invited me considered themselves 'the shepherds' of that city. I asked them if the other churches and pastors who were born again there knew about them and approved. In other words, suppose at the time of the Rapture they should find themselves going up with such men who never knew about them at all! Or, I also asked them, suppose a great crisis came, such as a depression or a nuclear war: what would happen then?"

"Well, what would?" Eleanore asked. I knew there was a twinkle in her eye, as she went on. "Guess we'd all have to go to the Word and do what God says, as we should have been, all along."

"True, Eleanore. But also, I heard myself telling those fellows something that afternoon I never thought of before. I said, 'The true elders will *emerge* in a time of crisis. God's mantle of power and His stamp of authority will be on them then in such a way that no one will question their right to lead.' Your pastor, mine, and many others will shine in that day for the rare gems God has been making them all these years, as well as many of the lay leadership around them. Given a nuclear war, we'll *find out* who the 'true shepherds' are."

"I believe that, Pat," she said, more seriously. "Even something *less* than nuclear war could do the job. Depression, famine, epidemics—any kind of hard times."

"Right. And there's a warning in the Word about 'lording it over God's flock,' isn't there? Doesn't it say something about 'being *examples* to the believers'? I think it's in I Peter 5."

I could hear the pages turning at the other end of the line, while I slipped through the back of my own Bible.

"Yes," she said finally. "Here it is in the third verse. The whole four verses at the beginning of the chapter are instructions to elders. How like the enemy to get some of the most valuable people in the current move of the Spirit derailed through disobedience to these principles! It frightens you. Are there any teachers warning against such dangers?"

"There are," I said. "In a recent prayer letter, the Episcopal rector Dennis Bennett issues a warning. Let me read it to you."

I was glad there is no such thing as televised telephones yet as I rummaged through my mess on the desk near the upstairs phone. Finally I found it, beneath a lot of unanswered mail, wincing as I thought of earlier years when I used to excuse myself for things like "intellectual clutter."

"Well, here it is," I said, grabbing the phone again. "I sure hope that lady wasn't right, years ago, who told me her idea of getting ready for the Rapture was cleaning out bureau drawers! Here, I'll read part of it to you. It's from the November '74 *Acts 29 Newsletter* of the Episcopal Charismatic Fellowship:

> "... I found the come-outers very busy! 'You must come out of your dead church, and join the new move of God!'; 'You need to get into freedom'; 'You need to do things in the New Testament way (that is, *our* way!). I recognize that there can be reasons that make it impossible for people to remain in their local church. If this happens, they should seek another church of their own denomination where the Gospel is being taught, or failing that, should move to a church as near to their own denomination as possible. Every time a person leaves his denomination to seek 'freedom,' he strikes a blow at the very thing God is trying to do.
>
> "If the outcome of the charismatic renewal is just another pentecostal denomination—and there are signs that just that very thing could be happening—the work will have to be done all over again... the 'come out' pressure is very strong, as are all the various extreme teachings about headship, submission, women's place, etc.,... as I spoke, people would say: 'It's good to hear someone who takes a moderate position on these things. We are being torn up by these extremes.'
>
> "Let's keep our heads—and our hearts! Let's remember that Jesus' *new* commandment is 'that you love one another, as I have loved you.'... (John 13:34.)"

"That's tremendous," Eleanore said. "There ought to be a book on all these things, to clear the confusion."

"There already is, and it's excellent. It's called *The Pendulum Swings,* by Bob Buess. Mother just sent it to me."

"You should tackle this in *your* new book, Pat," Eleanore commented.

"I will. Especially as it relates to the woman's role. All God's daughters need to hear some clear sanity from the Word on these matters, like that marvelous article of Loren

Cunningham's that was in the July *Christ for the Nations.*"

"Right. The one on 'True Women's Liberation.' I sent it to you, remember?"

"... Wow!" I interrupted. "We got kind of far afield from our discussion about our last five years in the charismatic movement, didn't we?"

"Not so far," she said, softly. "It takes time to learn all these things. The fruit of teaching takes time to grow and examine. Much has been good, but where the fruit is terrible, we have a right to examine facets of the teaching which are no good, and part with them. We must realize that people are still coming to your house for prayer meetings and deliverance, and young people are still coming to ours for prayer and ministry!"

"Yes, I do," I said. "And I guess as long as God keeps sending them, that will be the way it is. But He can stop either prayer meeting any time He wishes or it suits His purpose can't He? We're just the Lord's servants. We must be willing to be sent on any kind of errands or do any kind of thing He wants done—and *not* set up a new institution."

"Right!" Eleanore said. "I'm more grateful to the Lord than I ever was that He put us into evangelical Christianity and gave us a love for the Word. I appreciate His gifts, His healing and deliverance, and all the ways He shows us His love, but I'm surely glad to be closer than ever to the mainstream of the Body of Christ these days."

"Me too," I chimed in. "But I'd never trade this broadening He's given us, with fellowship with so *many* of the Body of Christ we didn't even *know,* especially Spirit-filled Catholics."

"Oh, I agree," she said. "Isn't it wonderful we don't have to give up any of our *old* family, even the dear fundamentalists who don't see the need for the gifts of the Spirit yet? But we also have a wonderful *new* family we'll be with forever in eternity."

"True!" I said. "Only God could bring about the unity of the Spirit we are experiencing today. It's so exciting. By the way, Eleanore, have you looked at the *clock?* We've talked for an *hour!*"

We both laughed, and the telephone conversation ended.

6 *"Letters" Worth Reading*

Someone has rightly said, "We are the only Bible many people read." The apostle Paul expressed this role of believers perfectly, when he wrote the Corinthian Church:

> You are our letter, written in our hearts, known and read by all men; being manifested that you are a letter of Christ, cared for by us, written not with ink, but with the Spirit of the living God, not on tablets of stone, but on tablets of human hearts. (II Corinthians 3:2,3.)

If then we are the epistles we should be, a beautiful message is conveyed to other hearts. They sense that God is love because He warms and loves them through us. They realize His fruit is joy when it bubbles up from our lives while others are falling apart around us. They notice His peace because we bring a balm of serenity into moments of chaos.

Recently I was sharing with a group that "the King's daughter is all glorious within" (Psalm 45:13). Afterward a girl said simply, "Did you know your face shone while you were talking? God showed me He means what He says, that way."

Since then I have looked at sisters and brothers in Christ with a new awareness of what the Lord wants for our lives. He would *show in person* what His Word says on paper. Not only is "one picture worth a thousand words," but also one good picture can stir an inner hunger *for* the Word. As the "Word became flesh" (John 1:14) in the incarnation, so God seeks to reveal His Word in mortal flesh today, by conforming His children to the image of His dear Son.

As I have prayed about what God's pattern woman is like, faces of real people I know have come to mind. Before I introduce them to you, however, let me quote my youngest son with a comment he frequently makes as he is being escorted to our first floor den for a spanking.

"Remember, Mom, nobody's perfect!"

Although none of these sisters in Christ has reached perfection, each evidences the King's power and victory in dynamic Christian service. Such women present eloquent, unspoken arguments to those who think a wife should only be an echo or a servant for the man in her life.

One Christian magazine pictured women in a variety of activities on its cover, *all in the home.* This subtle sermon smacked of male chauvinism to many. Some I met who had read it were almost ready to give up service in the King's harvest field.

Putting women under condemnation, making them feel that they are unworthy to do work for God, is the will of Satan. He is delighted with teaching that numbs and depresses the King's daughters, giving them a kind of evangelistic dystrophy. One pastor told me that his most effective teachers had all resigned from teaching the Bible, even to children, because of such devastating teaching. "And they are my best people," he commented.

Since fifty-three percent of the Body of Christ is made up of women, the devil could immobilize the church through such error! If your *own* body were fifty-three percent paralyzed, how much work could *you* do?

Such a concept is foreign to Scripture. Even the apostle Paul, lauded by chauvinists as their source for keeping women down, listed several ladies in chapter 16 of Romans as "workers in the Lord." There is nothing in the context to indicate that they were just frying the chicken, either!

Like *Sarai* (contentious), each one of us has been transformed by the King into a *Sarah* (princess) so that we might function like one. Born into the divine family of faith in Christ, our lives are not the product of self-effort. Rather, what we do gives powerful evidence to the presence of the Holy Spirit within.

However, in God's perfect plan, He must not only be *in* us, but a mantle of power *upon* us. The salvation verses in the Bible all use the Greek word *eis* or *into* for that function of the

Holy Spirit, coming within to regenerate and make us new. But the verses referring to the baptism in the Holy Spirit use *epi*: "But you shall receive power when the Holy Spirit has come *upon* you; and you *shall be* My witnesses both in Jerusalem, and in all Judea and Samaria, and even to the remotest part of the earth" (Acts 1:8).

Note that there is nothing optional about witnessing for the Lord Jesus Christ. No one is exempt from kitchen duty or any other kind. Like the Samaritan woman of John 4, we run to tell everyone we know about Him when He pours His living water through us.

The women I would like you to meet in this book are all of that kind. They know Jesus Christ as Baptizer in the Holy Spirit, as well as Lord and Savior. Four of them we shall meet right here in this chapter.

The first face which comes to mind is my mother's. How I thank God for the warm climate He gave our home through her! Loving, dynamic, and industrious, she is busier than ever now, in retirement with Dad. If you drop in on them when they're home, you might find Mother weeding in the garden, or Dad building a bulkhead down on the shore—driving piles and all. Their great joy is in sharing the good bounty God gives them with dozens of friends.

They have five acres on the Wye River of Maryland's Eastern Shore. While many folks their age are reminiscing about the past and nursing their aches and pains, Mother and Dad are back to the soil. They grow yard-long string beans, corn, mouth-watering canteloupes, raspberries, and Concord grapes. They can crab and fish from their boat or dock out front, but they refuse to shoot the geese which fly by the thousands overhead in fall and winter.

Mother still finds time and energy to work for God, however. Some time ago she started praying for a Christian bookstore in Easton. An on-fire new convert started it with Mother and another friend as volunteer sales help. Now the store is owned by a young couple who run it themselves, but Mother still tends shop for them whenever they want a respite.

Two days a week she teaches Bible studies: one to a few new converts, another to a group at the "House of the Pines," a local nursing home. Once Mother led a man in his nineties to the Lord; the next week when she returned, he was home in glory! Both studies give a grounding in the fundamentals of the faith.

"That's my ministry," Mother says firmly, "tending the spiritual nursery. When they get beyond that point, God sends them on to someone else."

Those who read *Out! In the Name of Jesus* will realize that Mother did not have a personal walk with the Lord when we left for Africa in 1962. What wonderful things God hath wrought in the intervening years!

Somehow Mother also finds time to cook the best meals I've ever tasted—homemade soup, crab cakes, spoon bread. And Dad's easily the happiest married man we know.

But all has not been continually rosy in Mother's Christian life. A few years ago her hands were gnarled, her wrists braceleted with strange knobs, and her whole body twisted and racked with the pain of rheumatoid arthritis. It was the first time in her life she had had a lengthy illness.

As she sought God for healing, she realized that she resented a certain in-law. What joy and victory she found as she forgave that one for every slight and unkindness! Then she began a daily routine of kicking her legs out, as she sat in her chair.

She would say, "Get out, Satan, in the name of Jesus Christ. You cannot have my body any more. You've lost your hold."

Today her wrists are as smooth as mine. The arthritis is nothing but a bad dream of the past.

"It was good for me, though," she says. "It taught me the awful danger of becoming prey to resentment, and I learned compassion for others. Now I don't lose patience with people who are sick."

The second one of the King's daughters who comes to mind here is a famous one who looks a little like my mother. I met Catherine Marshall during a never-to-be-forgotten week at *Guideposts* Writers' Workshop in Rye, New York.

Catherine and her second husband, Len LeSourd, met the "workshoppers" at an afternoon reception. Warm and compassionate, her youthful prettiness was mellowed from suffering. Every inch a lady, it was easy to think of her as

"Christy's" daughter. Surprisingly young looking, she might have been just a year or two past her life with *A Man Called Peter*. But especially touching was the loving tenderness she inspired in the eyes of a man called Len, as he watched her when her time came to speak to us.

Unassuming and approachable, Len LeSourd also made a big impression on all of us who where privileged to have won the week of training. He was executive editor of *Guideposts* at that time, and gave us a humorous, and sometimes moving account of the early years of the magazine.

Both LeSourds have that rare humility which God inevitably stamps upon those channeling His greatness.

At supper I had the unexpected treat of sitting directly across the table from Catherine. Talking with her was as invigorating as a college debate. A real thinker, she had a delightful way of lifting the conversation out of the realm of small talk. No wonder her books have a fresh wisdom that touches the heart! Rather than majoring in minors, she avoided the trite and obvious in her remarks and had a way of broadening those around her who otherwise might have maximized the mundane.

At one point we were discussing the moral and spiritual plunge of our nation during the past decade. With no hesitation she commented forcefully, "I believe the flood of evil can be traced back to the Supreme Court decisions removing prayer and Bible reading from our schools. God's hand is not on our nation in the same way it was when we honored Him in our halls of government and learning."

After dinner that night Catherine spoke to the workshoppers about her writing ministry. In her case it was clear that the gift God gave her with words had been laid back at His feet; she writes for His glory. A diligent worker, she revealed that she often rewrote a chapter many times before she was satisfied that it was good enough for God's service.

Years ago Stephen Olford, then pastor of the Calvary Baptist church in New York City, preached that discipline and determination were his two "flesh hooks" that kept his sacrifice of self bound to the horns of the altar. These, and the courage to be objective about one's writing, were emphasized by each of the truly great writers who taught us that week: Catherine and Len, Dick Schneider, Jamie Buckingham, and John and Elizabeth Sherrill.

Elizabeth Sherrill showed us many things that I would like to pass on to other daughters of the King. Almost a cameo of serenity and poise, "Tibby" was at the same time incisive and tactful in her approach to the competitive writings of the workshoppers. She had a knack of getting right to the point of our blunders, but her feminine grace muted the blows of the critique.

One day over coffee Tibby and I got into a lively discussion about the use of the term "Ms." She felt it was just a way of distinguishing "female" in the professional world, without having to know details about one's personal life. Her eyebrows went up when I mentioned that the term was a key one for the "women's lib" movement, a tool for the radical left.

That chat is as real to me today as the day we had it. We totally disagreed. Yet the challenge and joy of our argument lay in a simple fact. As redeemed womanhood, each of us saw her role stretching far beyond home and family. Yet each of us knew she must not fail *there,* either.

Home is the anvil on which God pounds His deepest truths into our hearts. If we *fail God* here, we fail Him everywhere. Yet note that I said, if we fail *God* here, not just "if we *fail.*" There are Christian women who cannot save their marriages in the cyclone of our times. Yet if they remain true to the Lord Jesus, preparing themselves for the heavenly marriage, He will never fail them. And what the world looks on, or even the church, as *failure,* may not be that at all. Such daughters of the King are divorcees Iverna Tompkins and Nora Lam.

In *Something More*, Catherine Marshall recounts God's continuing dealings with her on His anvil of family trials and sorrow. With the loss of two grandchildren, Catherine learned the secret of praise and trust in a whole new dimension.

The Sherrills' sensitive treatment of family life in *The Hiding Place* speaks volumes to me about their understanding and empathy with Corrie ten Boom. Only those who know how character is formed in a godly home could have written such a book—one of the truly great books of our time.

Looking back now, I see that God did many things to shape

my understanding of my role as His daughter and His writer that week. Precious experiences with all who were there melted into a memory of unity and fellowship. God is wanting His body to learn to function as we had to, a group of twenty-four studying under some of the greatest writers of our time. He is wanting to sharpen in us the art of discerning *His ways* with those He uses. Like Paul, who "sat at the feet of Gamaliel," we have special opportunities in life to sit at the feet of choice servants of the Lord. Thus we become better servants, ourselves.

During such times the prayer of George Mueller is safe and powerful: "Lord, help me to follow this person insofar as he follows the Lord Jesus Christ." That way I can follow him or her as far as either went with God, but not down any bypath into error or wrong emphasis.

From those I have mentioned and others whom the Lord has sent my way, I have learned the necessity of taking the Lord seriously, but not myself. Each of these believers seemed to have learned the art of a light touch toward self; they had gotten beyond the point of ego-centeredness. We all know people who must speak of *my* work, *my* happiness, *my* family; these had passed that stage. They were good listeners, able to throw themselves into the concerns of others with a holy abandon. This freedom from self, a heritage of the King's children, produces great thinking—the seed of worthwhile writing or work of any kind.

Every great person I have met has had this quality of *concern for others*. The old acrostic and formula for joy we teach the children is still true:

> Jesus first;
> Others second;
> Yourself last.

The fourth daughter of the King I think of is merry-hearted Marge Barnhouse, widow of Dr. Donald Grey Barnhouse. Regally radiant, Marge is Christian femininity at its finest. Still beautiful in life's autumn time, she sparkles with a holy joy through days that some would count drab.

Marge left Philadelphia in 1971. There she had many friends, happy memories, and much ministry. She returned to Albany because her mother, in her nineties and in a local nursing home, wanted her company. That's why Marge is here, and she takes her lot of frequent visits to the nursing home as one of privilege.

We in this part of the country are glad about the change, too, for now we can know Marge. Seldom have I met a woman so free of self-pity, so bubbling from within. She is an eloquent testimony to the truth that joy is independent of circumstances, but springs rather from a free flow of the Holy Spirit's unhindered work in one's heart. Someone once said, *"Happiness* has to do with *happenings; joy can overcome the worst of them."*

Widowed twice, each time suddenly, Marge has learned how to let God transform life's most bitter experiences into triumphs of His grace. Both husbands served the Lord. Marge herself has a teaching ministry, and a zest for living one seldom sees. Should the Lord tarry, it would be easy to picture Marge in her *own* nineties—still visiting nursing homes to comfort the elderly, still traveling about to disciple the daughterly!

Marge does not have to *wear* her womanly grace; it comes across from her personality as its very essence. Younger women flock to meetings or retreats where she speaks because they "read" the letter of her life accurately. They see pages of patience, sentences of spirituality, and phrases of fun-loving, non-phoniness.

Recently Marge and I had a talk about the life in the Spirit.

"I have never personally been given the gift of tongues," she said, "but whenever my mind disengages from whatever is occupying me I am aware of the surfacing to consciousness of what had been going on all along in the depths of me: 'psalms and hymns and spiritual songs, singing and making melody in my heart to the Lord' (Ephesians 5:19). But in English!"

"Did Dr. Barnhouse believe there were genuine gifts of the Spirit in our age?" I asked.

"He believed there would be a restoration of the gifts of the Spirit in the end times," she said. "The last year of my husband's life we were living on tiptoe, expecting the Lord at any minute. Since that time I have been so fascinated to see the Holy Spirit moving in power among the Lord's own. Of course there are extremes in any segment of Christianity: the extreme 'charismatic' who insists that unless you speak in tongues you are not 'in the Spirit,' and the extreme evangelical who says any speaking in tongues is 'of the devil.'

"You are a sailing enthusiast, Pat. You know you can set your sails to run with the wind, or manipulate the sails to use the wind to turn the boat, but you cannot change the wind! And if the wind changes, you'd better be on the alert: look to the set of your sails! Jesus said, 'the wind bloweth where it listeth' (John 3:8), and who am I to say He must blow only in a certain way? The mighty Wind of God—the Holy Spirit—is moving, and He cannot be hindered. So I am being very careful of the set of my sails."

"Praise Jesus!" I said. "I am wondering though, whether you have known times of discouragement in your present, rather circumscribed life."

"Oh, yes," she said. "About six months after I moved up here I went through a period where I felt very sorry for myself. One day I was grumbling on the inside, and of course the Lord heard me. Suddenly the thought came that *He* had been willing to wash the disciples' feet, and had told us to do the same for one another. The cloud lifted when I could say, '*This* is the washing of Your disciple's feet! Thank you, Lord. If You could do it, so can I.' "

"Marge," I said, "so many widows have lives like yours right now who know nothing of the victory you have. What do you say to them to help them change their attitude?"

"They are usually trying the wrong way," she answered. "When I was a young girl and lost my seventeen-year-old brother, I used to think *I* could 'keep my chin up.' I didn't have the Lord then, and it was the best I could manage. *Now* I find the easiest way to keep your chin up is to keep your eyes up—on the Lord Jesus Christ. Only when I used to look at myself would the loneliness threaten to overwhelm me. There is no feeling of being a poor, abandoned widow, no longer needed, when you look at Jesus, yield your total self to Him, and with the apostle Paul cry, 'Lord, what will You have me to do?' He will fill you with His joy, and keep you so busy there is no time for self-pity. Christian widows should try Titus 2:3-5 for starters. I tell them, 'If you honestly cannot teach, you can be a listening ear; you can pray; you can love.' "

After we hung up, it struck me that Marge Barnhouse has really learned the law of Proverbs 11:24: "There is one who scatters, yet increases all the more . . ." My mother, Catherine, Tibby, and Marge—all have learned the secret of scattering God's love and Word as they journey through life. Thus they have an endless supply left over for themselves as they continually bless others.

I remember how excited I was the day the Lord "opened" Matthew 16:9 and 10 to me. I always wondered why He made such a point of asking the disciples how many large baskets they had left over, after the miracle. Finally He showed me there were twelve baskets because there were twelve disciples. The ones doing the feeding of others from the precious bread of life have the most bounty of all! Instead of finding their store depleted as they continually give out to others, they have more and more there to give.

Years ago I noticed that a spiritual truth I got from teaching or from my own quiet time was *mine forever if I shared it*; if I kept it to myself, it could be gone within a few hours.

"Give, and it shall be given unto you" is a law written into the universe more solidly than gravity. It's also one of the "key three" secrets of the victorious disciple's life in Matthew 6:1-20. Jesus said, "*When* you give . . . *when* you pray . . . *when* you fast." He never considered the possibility of lives which did not include these mighty disciplines.

Although giving of our means is the primary thing spoken of here, giving of ourselves and our time also operates under the same laws to bring blessing. Let's be "letters" people read as giving, generous and outgoing.

Once I had a very unusual dream. It came after several weeks of such tremendous demands on my time that I felt almost trapped by the various calls of duty. In the dream I stood out on a hillside with hordes of people. It was a hot day, and I still remember the feeling of intense weariness I felt. Evidently I had been there for some time. Then I looked over at a very Jewish looking man with the most loving eyes I had ever seen. He just smiled at me; that was all. He was obviously working out there too.

When I woke up I knew I had seen the Lord, not as He is now in His glory, but as He was in His days of hard work among the people during His earthly life.

Peace filled my heart; His smile showed His approval. And that has made all the difference, ever since.

7 *Launching Our Sons*

That blowy March day in 1973 was a big one for us! A shipment of my first book had just arrived, quite flashy in their orange-red jackets. Soon every member of the family was buried in a copy of *Out! In the Name of Jesus,* and by suppertime the mood was hilarious.

"Hey, listen to this, guys. Mother's got an 'embarrassed fish' breaking into the 'enchanted silence' in chapter 12! What cornball stuff."

"That's nothin'. Have you read chapter one? It's positively pornographic!"

The only one who stuck up for me was Bob Stevens, a friend who was visiting for dinner. He took on Charlie, our eldest, eyeball to eyeball.

"Some *talk* and some *do*," he said firmly.

I could have hugged him.

During the next few days our home seemed like a hotel lobby. Friends and well-wishers phoned to comment on the book, as well as the usual people with problems. One young woman always managed to call either an hour after bedtime or just at suppertime.

One night she phoned just at six o'clock. I reached for the receiver with my right hand, a steaming bowl of green beans in my other. I motioned frantically to the children to turn off the burners and serve up the rest of the dinner, while I tried to give some attention to the hundredth call or so from this distraught girl. I listened for a few minutes, mumbled a brief prayer, and hung up wearily.

Charlie was standing in the doorway between the living room

and kitchen with his arms folded, watching me.

"Why don't you wake up, Mother?" he said as I bustled around, making final preparations for the meal. "Haven't you figured out yet that the devil is using people like her to *wear you down?*"

My eyes filled up as we all sat down at the table and Dick prayed. For a moment afterward, everyone was silent. I knew they all agreed with Charlie. I also realized he was right.

"Okay," I said finally, "what should we do about such people, and the telephone problem in general?"

"Limit them," Johnny said briskly. Our brilliant honor student usually had the answers, and they almost always were right. "Give them five minutes. No more. And tell them at the outset that's all you have."

"Also let them know how *I* feel about calls at bedtime and meal times," Dick added, grinning across at me. "Where are the rolls? Didn't I see you put some in the oven before that call?"

A tell-tale smoky whiff hit my nostrils, and I dashed for the oven door.

"Too late, Mommy," Billy said cheerfully, as I grabbed a pot holder and reached in for the burnt offering. "Are they too far gone to scrape like burnt toast?"

"Too far gone, Honey," I said, slamming the oven door quickly, and grimacing because of the smoke.

By now Dick had joined me with a bun warmer.

"Some of these are okay on the bottom," he said.

We walked back to the table and were just about to sit down when the phone rang again.

"Yes, this is she.... No, I cannot talk to you now, for we are in the middle of dinner as a family.... No, not that soon. We have family devotions right after dinner. Then I have to get my youngest son off to bed.... Not before eight.... Thank you. Goodbye."

"That's the way, Dear," my husband said, smiling. "Now eat your own dinner. I have a subject 'of general interest' to bring up to the family." (If you've read *Cheaper By the Dozen,* you'll remember that this was the standard by which the Gilbreth father judged every meal time conversation.)

"I'll bet it has to do with *Charlie,* then. He's sure of general interest these days. How many colleges have you applied to by now, Charlie—twenty?"

"Only five, squirt. Watch your tongue."

"Then where you gonna go, huh?"

"To a cave in Spain and study guitar under Segovia. Shut up and eat."

"We *will not* have that term, 'shut up,' in this family," I chimed in. "Any more of that and no more listening to music with ear phones for three whole days. What's of general interest, Dad?"

"The family vacation. This year I plan to take off the week the children have spring vacation, and go down to the outer banks of North Carolina. A fellow at work goes down there every spring, and he says it's great."

"What about visiting Grandma and Grandpa?"

"Yeah, I wanna go sailing. Can't we stop off there?"

"Briefly, maybe. But for a change we're going to give them a rest from the mob for a whole week this spring. And on the way we'll visit the Coast Guard Academy and Nyack College if Charlie wants to look them over."

"Great, Dad. Let's get out the atlas."

That was Johnny, of course. I knew that after he cleaned up the kitchen he'd have the rest of them sprawled out on the family room rug with two big atlases and an assortment of road maps. What could be more exciting during an ice storm upstate than planning a spring vacation in the South?

Not long afterward we arrived at our motel on the Atlantic coast near Morehead City. The pounding surf and sundrenched beach were delightful, but to my dismay we still had a cold breeze. My walks outside were brisk and brief; the young people and their Dad were made of heartier stuff. One day Beth Ann stayed in the surf for over two hours. (Most of the grownups lasted in it about two minutes!)

Charlie was glum all week as the pressure of an enormous decision weighed on him. Years of conflict between two major fields of interest—the sea and music—were demanding a final kind of decision.

One cloudy morning Johnny, Beth Ann, and Billy went fishing with Dad on one of the nearby wharves. Our vacation was nearly over, and Charlie had exactly four days to notify the Coast Guard Academy of his acceptance or rejection of his appointment. I suggested that he and I fast and pray together about this important step, since we had the place to ourselves.

I sat near the window, darning some socks. Charlie was sprawled out on a chair across the room. His Bible lay open on his lap. For a long time he said nothing. I thought he was asleep.

"Mother, what do you do when God says 'no' to what *you* want, and no other alternative appeals to you?" he said finally.

"You're talking about the music scholarship to the University of Southern California, aren't you?" I asked, squinting as I tried to thread a needle.

"Yup. That's all I wanted—to study guitar under Christopher Parkening. Since I didn't get that, I really don't want to go to the Coast Guard Academy *or* Nyack. Maybe I should just forget about school."

"I doubt that's God's answer," I said, pushing the needle and thread a little farther away to get a better focus.

"Why?"

"Because God gave you a good brain, and it's up to you to use it. Let's talk about our visits to the Academy and Nyack on our way down here. Did you have any definite impressions after either one?"

"Sure, but they were mostly negative."

"What was wrong with the Academy?"

"Too much math and science," he said, firmly. "If that's what it means to have a life at sea, I'm not interested."

"Anything worthwhile involves hard work," I said, pushing the needle and thread even farther away. My brows were knitted in great effort.

"Don't the arms come long enough these days, Mother?" Charlie said, chuckling. "Here, you want me to do that for you?"

"Nope. Just *got* it." I sighed gratefully, pulling the thread through. "Do you really think forcing yourself to take all that science and math would be too much?"

"I couldn't do it. But I don't know about music school, either. I never took any theory in high school, and I'm only self-taught in classic guitar."

"Well, the big thing about your music, in my opinion, is *why* you want to do it. Is it to prove some goal of your own, or do you really plan to use it to glorify God?"

"For the Lord, without any doubt," he said, glaring at me, and folding his arms on his chest.

"How can you be sure that's it?" I said, staring him down. "We've watched you listen to and play classical music for some time now, and are still wondering how this is going to tie in to your commitment to the Lord. How will He get glory from it?"

"If I do it 'as unto Him,' " Charlie said. Looking down at his Bible, he began leafing idly through the pages.

"Watch out for those stock phrases," I said. "They *can* be just a lot of religious talk. Do you know what the first commandment says?"

" 'You shall have no other gods before me,' " he said. "But what does that have to do with this?"

"Anything that means too much to us can be a rival for God in our affections," I said. "The whole trouble with this music interest of yours is that it's been something you have used to please *yourself*. I don't know of a time yet you've played for others or built up anyone for God with this talent."

"That's, uh, *true,* I guess," he said, grinning sheepishly.

"Then why not confess that to God as sin? Why not tell Him you want the music talent He has given you to be used for Him? Then I think your mind will be clear to make an objective decision about the next step in your life. Because it really boils down to two different *lives,* doesn't it? The sea or music."

Charlie said nothing. I closed my eyes and started praying in the Spirit, whispering. When I looked up he was praying, and for the first time all week he seemed to be at peace.

Suddenly the sunlight streamed into our room. As I looked out the window, the clouds had parted. Even the pounding surf looked friendlier.

"I'm going outside," Charlie said, standing up and reaching for his jacket. "The weather's changed and I'd like to take a walk on the beach."

For a moment I thought I might join him, but felt checked. I knew that he had to be alone with God. Whenever we come to a fork in the road it's like that. Others can pray and even fast with us, but ultimately the decision is up to us. The Lord has ways of dealing with us as we walk and talk with Him alone.

I watched the lonely figure disappear as he walked down the beach past the jetty.

It was hours before we saw him again, nearly suppertime. When he got back, he seemed much lighter-hearted. We knew the decision must be made, but no one asked him about it right away. Finally, during family devotions, the children could stand the suspense no longer.

"Charlie, *where* are you going to college?" Beth Ann asked, leaning over his chair from the back.

"To Nyack's music school," he said, matter-of-factly.

So the sea did not win. That was all there was to it.

After the younger children were asleep, his Dad, Johnny, and I wanted to know more.

"How did you come to that decision?" Dick asked. "Was it an impulsive thing, or are you really sure this is it?"

"Really sure," Charlie said. "Oh, I didn't see any neon lights or hear any words. I just prayed and talked it over with the Lord. But Nyack just kept coming to my mind. And with it came peace."

"Well, praise the Lord. We can't argue with that," I said, looking over at my husband. His disappointment showed in his face. As a graduate of King's Point and an ex-navy man, he had wanted a son to go to sea. Then there was the practical matter of turning down a four-year scholarship.

After the lights were out that night I lay awake a while trying to figure out God's dealings. Three words had come to my spirit while Charlie and Johnny were looking at the yacht squadron that day in New London: *I am working.* What did it mean? Had we made the trip to the Academy for no reason?

A year later I understood.

Johnny was at the same point in his own life. A three-year

graduate of high school, he applied to only two schools: Cornell and the Coast Guard Academy. He won full scholarships to both.

"I'm going to the Academy," Johnny announced one night at dinner.

"That's great, Johnny," Dick said, beaming broadly. "Think you can make the yacht squadron?"

"Not as a fourth class," he said, grinning back at his dad. "They don't allow it. But they do let freshmen on the sailing team. I'll try for that."

"And will you go all the way up to the royals on the *Eagle*?" Billy asked, jumping up and down in his seat.

"Do you get a cruise on the Eagle during swab summer?" Beth Ann asked.

"Sure. And you bet I'm going up," Johnny said.

Nothing would do at this point but bringing our book, *Men, Ships and the Sea,* to the table. There were "oohs" and "ahs" as Beth Ann cleared and all of us crowded around to look at the pictures. *National Geographic* had featured a cadet training cruise on the *Eagle,* a square-rigged bark. My "mother-heart" jumped as I saw shots of cadets climbing up the rat lines high above the sea.

Ruefully, I remembered someone telling me years ago, looking at the seascapes hanging everywhere in our home, "Anyone having seascapes all around will have at least one son go to sea." At the time that seemed fine; now I was not so sure.

That night I lay awake long after the clock had ticked past midnight. Memories crowded in from our harrowing Labor Day weekend in 1972.

We had taken the 21-foot *Venture* we then owned across the Chesapeake on a mild afternoon. After staying overnight on the western shore, we awoke to angry skies Saturday morning.

We had no good mooring for our boat where we were, so Dick decided to make the crossing, leaving the little children behind to be picked up by my dad in the car. He wanted to go just with Charlie, but I insisted if it was safe enough for him, it was safe enough for me. In the end Johnny went, too.

The Chesapeake Bay is nobody's mill pond in a stiff breeze.

The seas were choppy and the skies ominous when we left the western shore.

Small craft warnings were up, and I was at the tiller as we made our tumultuous way through a maze of sailboat races near the shore. Several of the racers were in trouble. We saw more than one *Star* with sails flat out against the water. Crew members of *Flying Dutchmen* and other light craft were hiking out to keep from capsizing.

Both of my arms ached as I fought the tons of force from sea and wind. When we had cleared the boat traffic, I turned the tiller over to Charlie, an expert sailor. I was exhausted.

Suddenly the four of us in *Venture* were all alone. An awesome quiet settled over us as we scrambled into our life jackets and rimmed the high side. *Venture* torpedoed through the writhing sea at a forty-five-degree heel; the wind was about thirty knots.

Rain began to come at us like needles fed sideways on a conveyor belt of wind. The waves were three to five feet high. A lone schooner under power, five times our size, was heading west toward us from the eastern shore. She rolled rail-to-rail as if she were trying to touch the waves with her mast.

Once we passed in front of a steamer coming north from Norfolk. Dick judged there would be plenty of room, but by the time we crossed her bow, that knife edge stood only a hundred yards between us and death.

Suddenly Johnny, then fifteen, began to shout and wave his arms at the merciless steamer.

"No, no!" he wailed—one desperate human voice against forces it could not control. Sea, wind, and engine noise from the freighter drowned his cry in their cacophony.

In a matter of seconds the crisis was over. We found ourselves waving to crewmen on the decks of our near-destroyer.

The rest of the trip was wild. When we turned into Eastern Bay, we had wind, current and waves against us. Dick and Charlie did the sailing. Johnny and I went below into the cabin. We all were soaked and shuddering from cold.

"Why are we out here, anyway?" Johnny shouted at me,

competing with the pounding against the hull. "Why doesn't the Lord still the storm?"

"God's way is not always to deliver us *from* the storm, Johnny," I said. "His main goal is to get us to trust Him."

Pushing my feet against the opposite seat in a vain effort to stay upright, I stretched to look through the porthole. The water around us was chaotic. A fifty-foot yawl nearby was pitching incredibly.

"But I think we're paying for our own foolishness," Johnny said, lurching toward the bow end of the cockpit as the *Venture* pitched suddenly. "We weren't supposed to be out here today or to *have* to trust the Lord here."

"If you can't trust Him here, you can't trust Him anywhere," I shouted back at him, as we each rallied to a sitting position again.

Now, as I lay in bed remembering that sailing adventure, I realized what stuff my son was made of. That day he discovered an area where he had shown weakness. Deep within I believe he determined to overcome it in God's strength.

Then I thought back to my last few weeks of pregnancy with Johnny when the Lord Jesus had saved me. I asked Him what to call my unborn child, and over and over He drew my attention to a phrase written by John, "the disciple Jesus loved." Finally I knew God wanted him to be "John," and Dick liked the name. I dedicated him to the Lord before he was born.

Once I heard Mrs. Elmer Thompson speak about her children. She and her husband had founded the West Indies Mission, and all of her six children were serving God when I heard her. As a new Christian I wanted her secret; I went up to her after the meeting.

"Why do you think all your children love the Lord?" I asked her. "Would you attribute it to your Christian home and proper balance of love and discipline?"

"Maybe five percent to that," she said, her eyes piercing mine. "Ninety-five percent I put to *prayer*. When you pray for each child by name, every day of your life, committing each one completely to God, *He* takes responsibility for how they turn out. And He is faithful!"

By God's grace, I followed her advice. It was the best I ever had. I also usually claim Ephesians 2:10 for each one. It's the foreordained plan of God we want for each child; not some willful idea of his own.

As I lay there thinking of God's faithfulness, I praised Him that Johnny was determined not to be a coward. He obviously wanted to know Jesus as Captain at sea, as well as Lord on land.

My eyes stung with silent tears as I thanked God for such sons; then I fell asleep.

8 Hazards of the End-Time Voyage

Our whole family has a love for the sea and for sailing. Thus I often think of our end-time spiritual journey as a great voyage. The Lord Jesus Christ is our Captain for the stormy weather ahead; everyone must obey His Word.

Our gospel ship seems like a great sailing vessel. The power to get us Home is the wind of God's Holy Spirit. In these days of darkening clouds before great storms, we leave our prejudices behind—climbing out of our lifeboats and joining the rest of the Body of Christ. As we preserve the unity in the Spirit, we find the sails trimmed just right for His wind. *Love,* one fruit of the Spirit, conveys the *power* of the Spirit for each new gust of circumstance.

Since much of the voyage in the larger vessel will be close-hauled and heeled over, *everyone must be on the high side.*

The *faith* that produces holy living is our life line, keeping us firmly attached to the ship. *Discipline* in the Word and prayer is our foul-weather gear, essential for survival in the worst of storms. Those living on the low side with neither of these risk being swamped when "scuppers are under."

Several imperatives are obvious in this analogy. Everyone must stay on the ship, trusting only in the blood of Christ and His resurrection to save them. No cry at sea is so terrifying as "man overboard!" In violent gales the huge waves and darkness often make it impossible to recover a lost one. Thus *no one* works on deck without a life line, leaving himself vulnerable to swamping by strange doctrines. Just as our Captain is the living Word, so our ship's chart is His written Word. He will never contradict Scripture; He warns us not to add to nor subtract from it (Deuteronomy 4:2; Revelation 22:18, 19).

One kind of seasickness we encounter on our voyage is celebrity-madness. If a well-known sports, political or entertainment figure who professes Christ says something, millions think it must be so. Even if his teaching does violence to Scripture, soon many follow him, willy-nilly, like lost children under the spell of the Pied Piper. Such leaders only confuse people, according to John Conlan, U.S. Congressman from Arizona.

This modern Daniel abhors compromise. He believes he must vote Biblically and support only those programs for which he will not be ashamed when he stands before his Lord. At the judgment seat of Christ he knows he will account for his public life as well as for his private and church life. He prays, dreams and works toward a day when born-again men and women, dwelling in God's Word, will be *salt* in our government. He urges many to obey God's "Go ye" into the political part of "all the world" (Mark 16:15).

The seasick ones following non-Biblical celebrities are eating a dangerous diet. Of it Jesus said, "Beware of the leaven of the Pharisees, which is hypocrisy. But there is nothing covered up that will not be revealed, and hidden that will not be known" (Luke 12:1, 2).

We would not expect either babies or deranged persons to teach in our universities. In the same way it is folly to expect untrained believers who scarcely have begun to drink the milk of God's Word to feed others. Scripture is called milk for several reasons. First of all, the baby cannot live without it. Second, the milk must be drunk every three of four hours. Healthy babes in Christ feed on Scripture constantly.

Unfortunately, some widely publicized converts never dwell in the Word. Thus the errors from their old life cling to them. They know little of the renewing of their minds through displacement with God's thoughts. Yet some are teaching and sharing testimonies with millions.

At the judgment seat of Christ, every one of us will be accountable to God. Having taught others anything but God's Word will prove disastrous in that day. God will not wink at nor overlook such sin. No wonder James says, "Let not many of you become teachers, my brethren, knowing that as such we shall incur a stricter judgment" (James 3:1).

Other seasick ones are not following a "name" but a "fad." Here the error itself is the attraction. The charismatic movement has seen many of these passing fancies. Usually they start out soundly, but the devil often succeeds in getting God's people pulling so hard in a tug of war against worldly evil that they fall back into fanaticism.

Such fads in recent years have been an over-emphasis on demons, headship, and submission. Frankly, I still believe in the deliverance ministry and would not be able to function for God if He had not delivered me. But I deplore the charlatans who think casting out evil spirits will bypass the necessity for a disciplined, holy life. Only those who walk in the light, in the will of God, have any hope of freedom from demonic oppression. *God sets us free to do His thing, not ours.*

Another important truth in God's Word is that we are all under authority. We must submit to Jesus as Lord and to His Word as our final rule for faith and practice. Then we also fit into a chain of command here on earth, according to divine order. However, we never get to the place where obedience to man nullifies obedience to God's Word. When man and God disagree as to what we should do, like Peter, "We must obey God rather than man" (Acts 5:29).

Fellow sailors on our end-time voyage who have swallowed error fads constantly are leaning over the lee-side of the vessel to regurgitate them. They are too sick to help others, and they drain the energy of God's servants in their need-oriented self-centeredness. If they fail to turn away from their errors, they always will be part of the problem rather than part of the answer, on our ship!

Tom Micklas, a young Coast Guard officer and our son in the Lord, told us this fascinating account of his only serious bout with seasickness. During his last cadet summer cruise he was navigator on a cutter traveling through the North Sea during a gale. Some of the automatic equipment on the ship had failed, and he was forced into long hours of strain and work under grueling conditions. He never ate during the crisis. Thus when the violent rolling of the ship increased, his body lacked its normal equilibrium. He soon became so sick that, for the first time since he became a Christian, he wanted to die.

"But if I had eaten, I would have been all right," he concluded.

My guess is that many readers are reeling through dark days and wanting to die. You need to start *now* in the regular, systematic study of the Word. (See *Out! In the Name of Jesus* or *Using Your Spiritual Authority* for a workable plan, if you do not already have one.)

Most would not dream of attempting their daily routine without food. Bodies cry out to be fed. Yet one of the tragedies of famine is that starving men can be near death without realizing it.

Our innermost spirit, where God's Spirit dwells, also cries out for proper food. What do we give it? The slop of violence, immorality and occultism spewed forth from television? The sawdust of secular humanism from satanically controlled media? The gruel of gossip and self-pity shared with other seasick ones on the telephone? The husks of hilarity from escapist-reading and joking?

As the Lord convicted me of the "tele-sins"—especially the telephone—I found He means what He says in Proverbs 10:19: "When there are *many* words, transgression is unavoidable, but he who restrains his lips is wise." (*She* who restrains, too!)

For almost two years after my first two books were published, my typewriter was silent under the sheer tyranny of time. Satan cleverly had me substituting the *good* for the *best*. Hundreds of counseling phone calls made it impossible for me to get back to my writing ministry. Piles of letters came in which I tried to answer.

Finally I had to make a choice. My time with the Lord and my family had to come first and second, in that order. *Third* would come the teaching ministry, and *priority would go to writing books and articles*. God gave me peace. In this way He could help far more than if I allowed myself to be bogged down in the mire of correspondence and phone calls. Even recently, with secretarial help, these ground rules remain unchanged. Is there still some unanswered mail? Yes. Do we still keep phone calls short? Few more than five minutes. *Does it work?* Yes!

It was exciting to pray for the ingredients of a good

counseling phone call that would encourage seasick ones onto a good diet in the Word of God. The recipe turned out to be relevant Scripture passages (more than he or she could possibly read in a week), the titles of good books on the subject at hand, and prayer for the sufferer at the end of the call. This intercession punctuates a phone call easily.

Often I set a time limit on such calls by saying, "I have five minutes. What can I do for you?"

In 1974 I spoke at a fall retreat for women at The Barn in Mercer, Pennsylvania. After I shared my "steps to shorter phone calls," a perplexed girl came up to me.

"I think that's harsh and unyielding," she said. "Suppose some people need more time?"

"Then the Spirit of God will let you give more, with peace in the process. Just don't let the long be the *habit*, that's all."

"But that's my whole point. I disagree with you. I think *most*, if not *all* people who call me need lots of time. They would be hurt and disillusioned if I failed to listen."

"Perhaps. But have you ever asked a caller if she's spent as much time on her knees pouring out her problem to God, as she has on the phone with you?"

"No! I think that's being nervy and judgmental."

"Then you believe in sloppy-*agape*."

"What do you mean by that?"

"Confusing sentimentality with love. Knowing better than God what's good for a person. You see, divine love, real *agape*, loves the person enough to want God's best for him. Abiding in that kind of love enables you to show great compassion for the *person* while you set yourself squarely against the sin that is destroying him. It puts fire in your prayers to say, as I often do for my children, 'Lord, do what you have to do to make them servants of Yours who will be true to You, no matter what. And I trust You for the grace not to wince or put my hand out to stop You in the process.'"

"Why, I think that's *terrible*," my young friend said. "That doesn't sound like love to me. I want people who come to me to find a shoulder they can cry on."

"Sometimes that's necessary," I retorted. "But you have to be careful."

"Why?"

"Well, God wants people depending on Him, not on you. Be careful you don't catch a disease like 'ministry-hunger.' It's just one step beneath the matriarchal complex that must run other people's lives."

"And what's the root of *that*?" she asked, lifting her eyebrows in a puzzled way.

"Can be pride, rebellion, witchcraft, or even a lesbian spirit. Sometimes it's a combination of several of these things at once."

"How did you ever come to such outlandish conclusions?"

"Watching a few women maneuver in an area where we once spent a summer vacation." I reached for my Bible and pulled over a folding chair. "Why don't you sit, too? This will take more than five minutes."

She grinned when I grinned, this time, and dragged another chair through the straw on the ground.

"What were they up to?" she asked, now thoroughly curious.

"Trying out some novel ways to get guidance from God. They'd sit in circles and ask questions of the Lord, always requiring the answers to be inner words or 'leadings.' Some used the Bible almost like a ouija board, opening it at random for answers.

"One gal taught that you must have a direct line to God, and it would be a two-way conversation. The whole process could be speeded up, according to this seer, by having a *prayer partner*. This person would be someone of the same sex with whom you were spiritually attuned. Such pairs were to spend *hours* with each other, usually alone.

"One husband of a former prayer partner of the 'seer' told me he always felt like an intruder when he interrupted their prayer times. He also told me he became very uneasy about their relationship, but he could not explain why."

"How did his wife ever wise up?" my young friend asked, all interest, now.

"God did it. He began to convict the wife of the wasted time. And one day while she was reading the Bible, she sensed a sharp warning. The passage was the one in I Samual 28, where Saul consulted the medium."

"How about the 'seer'? Did she have a regular time in Scripture, too? I mean, this story scares me. Just how far can Satan go in deceiving someone who is trying to lead a consistent Christian life?"

"You have two questions here," I answered, slowly. "First, the 'seer' did not believe in the authority of the Bible as the infallible Word of God. She felt only those portions were God's Word which spoke to *you*. You were free to toss out anything which did not hit you just right.

"Now in answer to the *big* question. I don't think Satan has any power at all to deceive those who *will* to do the will of God. Look up John 7:17 and read it from my New American Standard Bible."

The eager young girl leafed through her Bible and found the verse.

" 'If any man is willing to do His will, he shall know the teaching, whether it is of God, or whether I speak from myself.' Oh, I see it! If someone is willing to do God's will, he'll have real direction on what's true and what's deception. Is that right?"

"Right on!" I said. "The ex-prayer partner had a deep love for her husband as well as the Word of God. She was committed to make her marriage work. But the other woman was a rebel at home. She merely endured her marriage, and was constantly forcing herself into a dominating role over the lives of other women. What she wanted from these gals was something akin to *worship*. I am convinced she was bound by a lesbian spirit, but I doubt she knew that. She rationalized all of her behavior—even using her husband as a front man for her critics."

"What kind of man was her husband? A real Milquetoast?"

"No. That's what makes this story so sad. He was a decisive, likable fellow, but lacking in knowledge of Scripture. I think he saw his role as 'defender of the prophetess' rather than head of the house. There is a world of difference between these two."

"There certainly is. But if he tried to function as head, do you think that woman would ever submit, anyway? I bet he thinks it's hopeless."

"Possibly." I looked out the barn door which, slightly ajar, was letting in the sunlight and brisk fall air. "But I think

God will *require* him to establish his authority there, even if it brings about a blow-up of the marriage."

I walked over to a bench by the wall and got my sweater. As I struggled into it, my young friend joined me.

"But isn't he right to avoid a showdown in order to save the marriage?"

"Better the earthly marriage broken than not to be ready for the heavenly one," I said, quietly. "Besides, there was havoc from that woman's teaching and effects upon other people's lives. She'll be held accountable for all that rotten fruit."

"What do you mean by rotten fruit?"

"She caused strife and division in the Body of Christ throughout her area," I said, buttoning up my sweater. "She lured other believers away from trust in the Bible, and she made subjective guidance her standard, instead.

"Others throughout the nation are falling into similar traps. It would be unusual if we didn't have some right here at Mercer, using such methods of waiting on God. And if they start from the same kind of rebel base, they are heading toward the same dangerous shoals that the women in this guidance circle were.

"It all boils down to who sits on the throne of our hearts: Jesus Christ or self. Eventually, our actions will make it abundantly clear."

"But isn't that salvation by works?" my friend said, her face reddening with defense-of-the-faith fervor.

"Nope. We are saved by the blood of Christ, His finished work on the cross. But after we are born again we must be 'doers of the Word, and not merely hearers who delude themselves' (James 1:22)."

"But what of carnal Christians who accept Christ, then do as they please?"

"Thank God He does not allow us to judge. But the first three chapters in Revelation give the bright promises to *overcomers*. So why settle for anything less?"

"You mean there will be *degrees* of blessedness in heaven?"

"Of course. The Bible teaches that in the parable of the talents (Matthew 25), and in the section on the judgment seat of Christ."

"Are there several passages which refer to that? I thought it was just II Corinthians 5:10."

"Good girl. That's one of them," I said. "But open your Bible to I Corinthians 3:10-15. That's an important one."

My young friend settled down on a nearby chair again, and opened her Bible. I went for my coat and notebook. It was getting late. We had been there all day; I had spoken twice.

"Time to call it quits," I said.

"Oh, I realize that," she said, glancing up from her reading. "How can we know what wood, hay and stubble is in our lives? After all, if some works are going to be burned up some day, shouldn't we part with them now?"

"Seems sensible. Apply the three-fold test to what you're doing. One: Is it Scriptural? Two: Is the Lord Jesus—or some human being—glorified by it? And three: What is the fruit of it? Remember, *He* said bad fruit, bad tree; good fruit, good tree."

"But what *is* fruit?" The young brow wrinkled.

"The result of actions taken. The Bible speaks of two kinds of fruit: The fruit of the Spirit in Galatians 5, and the fruit of the womb in Psalm 127. You should be able to see the fruit of the Spirit in the life of the one ministering and also in his or her children or followers."

My young friend started shaking her head, giving a long whistle.

"Then you won't even allow a godly man a single rebel among his kids?"

"Well, maybe one—for a while. But if he's doing what he should the young person will come around some day. God says, 'Train up a child in the way he should go; even when he is old he will not depart from it' (Proverbs 22:6). That allows for middle-year rebels."

"Isn't that a rather harsh way to judge a person's ministry?"

"Not at all. Home is the laboratory where we work God's principles into our lives before passing them on to others. Christians who are moving in the Spirit have a right to claim Acts 2:39 and 16:31."

"Why don't they, sometimes?"

"Unbelief and disobedience in meeting God's conditions, usually. Remember, Israel wandered in the wilderness for forty years instead of entering the promised land. Numbers 13 and 14 make it clear that they listened to the ten spies who were walking *by sight*, rather than *by faith*. They refused to believe Caleb and Joshua who knew God would conquer all enemies—giants or otherwise. By the way, those ten doubting spies paid an expensive price for teaching God's people to doubt Him. They were killed immediately in a plague."

I put my coat on and buttoned it up. My young friend jumped up and gave me a bear hug. I realized I hadn't even learned her name.

"Thanks so much, Pat. Especially for giving me more than five minutes!"

We both grinned as we headed for the door.

"Oh well, the best of man-made rules have to go once in a while. Otherwise we'd all turn into legalists."

"But only once in a while," She laughed as she said it. "Without a few guidelines, I guess we'd be looking for 'subjective guidance' about whether to get up and get dressed in the morning! So long, and God bless you."

9 *In the Footsteps of Three Mary's*

Some of my favorite moments have been spent looking out across the Wye River from my parents' dock. Less than a half mile wide, this body of water on Maryland's eastern shore is one of the few unspoiled places left in our busy world. One can see Wye Island just as it has been for hundreds of years: no honkey-tonks, cabins or condominiums mar the picture.

The reason this country paradise is unspoiled is that the owners of the island still keep it as a sanctuary for wildlife. Canadian geese by the millions find a safe place to winter there. Those shot during the hunting season have been lured by plowed fields onto the mainland. The sensible ones stay on the island, running no such risk.

There geese and ducks explore the lush groves and medley of meadows, perhaps even venturing near the river when it is free of hunters lurking in duck blinds. Stately swans are bolder, swimming openly in the tree-lined coves. Do they know they enjoy immunity from murder guaranteed by law? Probably not. At any rate, they function just as God intended, bobbing for fish more deftly than youngsters for apples. Sometimes a mother swan will paddle near the shore, with four or five babies behind her. The tiny webbed feet may spank at the easy river current twice as often as hers, but they manage to keep up. Thus the Almighty's pattern continues: The young learn His ways from those who already know them.

So the Lord has given countless pictures in His Word of those who have walked the path of faith before us. Some of these saints have "grown on me" after years of dwelling in the Scriptures. Especially precious are the three Mary's of the New Testament. Like old roses and honeysuckle on the Wye River bank in springtime, their lives shed a special fragrance through the divine record. The King wants us to pass this sweet scent on to our generation through His daughters, today.

First, Mary of Nazareth. A poor girl, she came from the wrong town, "the other side of the tracks." Her only mark of distinction was her lineage. A direct descendant of Israel's great king, David, perhaps she pondered why the Scriptures promised his seed would reign forever. Herod, the usurper, ruled Galilee in her day. Thus she had to live her life in territory ruled by an enemy despot. God's people were oppressed through Satan's puppet. A Jew of no rank, with no wealth to warrant her betrothal to a famous man, Mary was a nobody in Nazareth.

But not to God! When the angel Gabriel appeared to her to tell her she had been chosen to bear the Son of God, he said, "Do not be afraid, Mary; for *you have found favor with God*" (Luke 1:30).

Not a word of fear or rebellion escaped her lips. There was no cringing at the cost of ignominy and shame which would be hers; yet whispered slander and misunderstanding were to be her lot for a lifetime. Who would ever believe her tale? Not even her fiance. A virgin pregnant? Impossible. Except with God.

Little more than a child herself, probably in her teens, Mary knew what she was. More important, she knew who God is: "My soul exalts the Lord, and my spirit has rejoiced in *God my Savior*. For He has had regard for the *humble estate of His bondslave* . . ." (Luke 1:46-48).

Gentle Mary. Simple enough to accept God's will, however hard, she could believe Him for good from it. Not ambitious like Eve, she never bought the serpent's lie that she would be "like God." Not nagged by self-pity like Naomi, she never whined, "Call me Mara, for the Almighty has dealt very bitterly with me" (Ruth 1:20). Not laughingly skeptical like Sarah, she never said, "*Shall* I indeed bear a child?" (Genesis 18:12), but rather, "*How* can this be?"

Later her cousin Elizabeth said, "And *blessed is she who believed* there would be a fulfillment of what had been spoken to her by the Lord" (Luke 1:45).

Tiny Mary towers over faith giants in all ages for what she believed—without complaint, without reluctance, without doubt. No wonder she could say, anointed of the Holy Spirit,

"From this time on all generations will call me blessed" (Luke 1:48).

Next, we come to the woman who understood Jesus better than any of them, Mary of Bethany. One of two sisters and a brother whose home always was open to the Savior, we meet her first where we see her last—at His feet: loving Him, listening to His Word, appreciating Him for Who He is, perhaps not even asking Him anything. No wonder Martha was jealous!

Probably it was a hot day, the worst possible time for bothering about a big meal. Yet Martha reasoned that the Lord must have the very best. Surely He would appreciate her good works on His behalf. But that Mary, just sitting there, gazing up at Him. The nerve of her! Why didn't she grab a dish towel and get out there and help?

She hated to interrupt, but what would *you* do?

" 'Lord, do You not care that my sister has left me to do all the serving alone? Then tell her to help me' (Luke 10:40).

"But the Lord answered and said to her, 'Martha, Martha, you are worried and bothered about so many things; but only a few things are necessary, really only one; for Mary has chosen the good part, which shall not be taken away from her'" (Luke 10:42).

It wasn't, either.

A week before Calvary the scene was so much the same: Martha still serving, Lazarus reclining at the table, Mary at the Lord's feet. But oh, what had happened in the interim. Lazarus had died and been buried. His body had reeked with four days of decay when Jesus came. What noise the mourners made! No wonder He cried out with a loud voice, "Lazarus, come forth" (John 11:43).

But not before He wept when He saw Mary weeping. Although He is the Resurrection and the Life, He feels with compassion the anguish of those He loves in their moments of loss. Mary knew Him so well. Why did she not know He would turn her mourning into dancing?

I think *her problem then was that she was not at His feet*. He had been away, and delayed when she sent for Him. She did not know how to function without the consciousness of His presence. But she had to *learn*. As much as the Lord loved her,

He knew a much greater sorrow lay ahead. Soon she would have to dwell in His presence by faith, for His physical presence would be gone for good.

Yet His perfect humanity understood her grief, just as His incarnate deity would soon turn it to joy. What verses better reveal the God-man than "Jesus wept" (John 11:35) over against "Lazarus, come forth!" (John 11:43).

Try to imagine the yearning, loving heart of Mary as she tried to thank Him for raising her brother. What could she say? What could she give Him? Was there *any* worthy way she could show her love for Him?

She knew, you see. She realized He soon must die. He recognized she was preparing him for burial. And in some moment of searing insight she found her answer for a suitable gift.

What matter that the spikenard ointment cost her a year's wages? Lifetime wages, her life itself, would never be good enough; this gift was a mere token of her love. *The secret of Mary of Bethany was that she knew something of the infinite worth of Jesus.* She loved Him; in the mighty waterfalls of His own love, rather than in the trickle of her own capacity.

How the legalists hate this last vignette of Mary on her knees before Jesus! What uneasiness her wiping the ointment on His feet with her hair causes them. Down through the ages some side secretly with Judas, thief and betrayer, who said, "Why was this ointment not sold for three hundred denarii, and given to poor people?" (John 12:5).

Such folks would be misfits in heaven. There, all praise and activity centers on the Lord of Glory. Like Mary of Bethany, we shall love and love and find our hearts infinitely stretched for loving. Praise God for the privilege *now* of sitting at His feet and hearing His Word; then spilling out our lives for Him.

Is it costly to spend and be spent for the Lord Jesus? Not really. What we give Him now of ourselves and everything we possess will be applied to our eternal account with enormous interest. The only truly costly path will be holding back from Him what is rightfully His.

Remember that He bought us with the price of His own blood. This is far more than religious talk or theological doctrine. In plain language, *He* owns us now, not we ourselves.

The owner has a right to do what He wishes with His own. Once we are fully determined to be His, and have no other master, we will be happy to lay all we have at His feet.

Do we *yet* understand that "He died for all, that they who live should no longer live for themselves, but for Him who died and rose again on their behalf" (II Corinthians 5:15)?

Mary of Bethany did. The Lord Jesus accepted her willing sacrifice and said, "Wherever this gospel is preached in the whole world, what this woman has done shall also be spoken of in memory of her" (Mark 14:9).

Last, let us follow in the footsteps of the King's daughter of Easter morning, Mary of Magdala.

Her claim to fame a dubious one, she never met the standards of the status-seekers. She followed Jesus simply as one "from whom He had cast out seven demons" (Mark 16:9). Everywhere she went, they must have said, "See her? She used to be demon-possessed. You should have seen her when she raved. What a madwoman!"

Yet her life had more focus, more purpose, than that of all her critics. She lived for the sake of her Deliverer; it was as profoundly simple as that. Traveling with other women "who were contributing to their support of their private means" (Luke 8:2,3), she doubtless helped with the cooking and stayed in the background. One can picture her washing the Savior's feet when He was weary at the end of a journey and bringing Him a cool drink of water from a well.

Then suddenly her world crashed to an end at Calvary. It seemed then as though the Light she lived for had been snuffed out. Would the swirling powers of Satan envelope her again? Would she be swallowed up in darkness?

Resurrection morning, spices in hand, she went with Mary, the mother of Jesus, and Salome, to anoint the hastily buried body of Jesus. She was with the other women, yet not with them. We find her weeping near the empty tomb after Peter and John have raced away to tell others.

Yet she was not alone. Two angels sat where the Lord's corpse had been, and behind her a Person stood. As she turned around, He spoke:

" 'Woman, why are you weeping?'

"Supposing Him to be the gardener, she said to Him, 'Sir,

if you have carried Him away, tell me where you have laid Him, and I will take Him away' " (John 20:11-15).

Then He said that thing which identified Him to her as no physical semblance ever could. That word has rung down the ages, igniting faith in all who want a personal relationship with the Living God.

"Mary!" (John 20:16).

She had heard Him call her name dozens of times before. No one else ever said it quite like He did. The love, the tenderness, the gentle rebuke at her doubt—all were wrapped into that word that clothed her world with light again. No need to fear the powers of darkness now! They would never come back! Jesus had banished them in His death, and the very atmosphere was charged with His life.

"Teacher!" she said to Him in Hebrew, reaching out to touch Him.

"Stop clinging to Me; for I have not yet ascended to the Father," he replied, "but go to My brethren, and say to them, 'I ascend to My Father and your Father, and My God and your God.' "

No lingering, now! How she ran, breathless, to the disciples. An awe settled over them as they saw her. Her eyes had an electric quality to them, fired by love.

"I have seen the Lord," she said, simply.

Seen Him? Ah yes, and far more than that. Heard Him call my name, knowing now that He still loves me, she could have said. *Imagine His incredible love, appearing first to me, Mary of Magdala, formerly the madwoman. All the demons of hell could be arrayed against me now, and it would make no difference. The Lord Jesus is alive, and He's with me. He calls me by name and keeps me safe. Mary of Magdala. Think of it! Least of His daughters, nothing to make me worthy of His life and love. He's set me free and I shall never go back into darkness. Mary the bound, now Mary the free. Do you hear, people? Free, free, free!*

Yes, Mary, we hear. We hear as we listen to a robin's call from a bursting forsythia in sudden spring. We see your joy like watching a crocus peep up through the snow. We feel your wonder at hearing Jesus call your name. And resurrection morning happens in us when we hear Him call ours.

Can we ever be the same after that? Impossible! Members of the royal family, we must live as children of the King. Freed from the tyranny of the trite, our whole life prepares us for a wedding with the royal Bridegroom.

> "Listen, O daughter, give attention and incline your ear;
> Forget your people and your father's house;
> Then the King will desire your beauty;
> Because He is your Lord, bow down to Him.
> And the daughter of Tyre will come with a gift;
> The rich among the people will entreat your favor.
> The King's daughter is all glorious within;
> Her clothing is interwoven with gold.
> She will be led to the King in embroidered work;
> The virgins, her companions, who follow her,
> Will be brought to Thee.
> They will be led forth with gladness and rejoicing;
> They will enter into the King's palace." (Psalm 45:10-15.)

Like brides throughout the ages, we are getting ready. Our wedding gown is different, though, from those of contemporary culture. The white of Christ's own righteousness, given to us as the gift of His love, is *interwoven with gold*. Job could say, "But he knows the way I take: when He has tried me, I shall come forth as gold" (Job 23:10). Peter knew that we must rejoice, not tremble, in trials, since we are purged and proved by them. Thus our *"faith, being more precious than gold which is perishable, even though tested by fire, may be found to result in praise and glory and honor at the revelation of Jesus Christ"* (I Peter 1:7).

We can trace our steps to triumph through these magnificent Scriptures. *Listening to* the King, we incline our ear to His voice, like Mary of Bethany, *bowing down to Him*. Like Mary of Nazareth, we come in full surrender to His will, acknowledging Him as both Savior and Lord. Like Mary of Magdala, we are freed from bondage and *led forth with gladness and rejoicing*.

All glorious within, we can never be tarnished from troubles without. Indeed, God spins new gold thread for our wedding gown from each trial!

10 Doormat or Disciple?

One morning the phone rang just after the children had left for school. I heard a familiar, if weary voice. It was a friend in another city whom I shall call "Grace." (That is appropriate anyway, since God has given her much of His grace since she met Him.)

"Pat, I've put the submission teaching fully to the test," she told me, "but the *fruit* is vile. I can sense the grieving of the Holy Spirit within. Stew is becoming more arrogant daily, and he seems to relish grinding his heel down on me as his doormat. Worst of all, he has gone back to drinking and running around with that wild crowd again."

"I'm sorry to hear that, Grace," I said. "But are you *sure* it's the submission teaching? How have you been interpreting it?"

"Well, I've stopped going to prayer meetings unless he actually says he wants me to go. I fix his meals at whatever crazy hours he shows up, and I don't mention the inconvenience. I won't allow the children to criticize him, and have been defending him to them, even when I know he's wrong. But last night the police brought him home drunk at three a.m. The children woke up, with all the commotion. They saw him like that, and the disgust of the police who left him here. This morning they asked me if the Lord Jesus is happy with Daddy and our home right now. I didn't know what to say to them. What *could* I have said?"

Grace's voice broke, and she began to weep softly at the other end of the wire.

"I think I'd switch gears," I said finally, after a brief, silent prayer.

"What do you mean by that?"

"Well, when something isn't working, you don't keep it up.

As far as I understand the Scripture, submission to a man is 'as unto the Lord.' In other words, whatever the Lord can honor in that man's behavior and demands is proper for submission. Whatever goes contrary to the Lord and His Word must *not* be yielded to, or we become guilty of yielding to sin. Romans 6 makes it clear that this is a deadly business."

The crying had stopped.

"Pat, that's the way I've seen this thing from the first. But you cannot imagine the pressure put on all the women in this area to submit to *everything* their husbands say or do. Certain teachers have come from out of town, and tapes of others are circulating. They are teaching something which brings forth *bondage,* not freedom. As I looked in the mirror this morning I was forced to admit to God that I am a sorry shell of the person I was when I first met Christ. My joy is gone, and there is torment written all over my face. Worse yet, there is not the sense of the Lord's presence in my life I knew before we all 'knuckled under' to this new teaching."

"Then scrap the extremism," I said. "Confess it as sin to the Lord, like any other sin, and affirm again that *He* is Lord of your life, and *His Word* is your standard."

"That's no problem," Grace answered, sighing with relief. "But what about changing this situation here in our home so the devil does not continue to run it?"

"Right!" I agreed. "Bind the evil spirits influencing Stew's behavior *daily* in the name of Jesus Christ. But do it just before he comes home. Let the other people he has to deal with during the day cope with him just as he is. That way he is going to have to face up to his spiritual need, sooner or later."

"I *have* been binding the spirits," Grace said thoughtfully, "but I've done it only occasionally—usually in the morning. I'll try this daily way. But I can tell you one thing. This won't stop *all* his nonsense, because he's pulled some dillies on the days I bound the demons."

"Then you can be sure his kicking up his heels is willful, deliberate behavior, and not just a result of bondage. Don't forget that we human beings have free will. We cannot bind *that.*"

"All right, I get the point," she said. "But what would *you* do if you had my situation?"

"I'll tell you, on one condition," I answered.

"What's that?"

"That you take what I say as exactly that: simply what *I'd* do—not necessarily advice for you."

"Okay shoot—on that basis."

"I'd take off for a few days and not let him know where I was."

"With the children?"

"Yes. A woman who'd leave her children isn't worth her salt. Don't ever be guilty before God of something like that."

"Pat, this is fantastic!" Suddenly Grace's voice was alive and joyful. "This is *exactly* what came to my mind when I prayed about it this morning. Your idea is nothing more than confirmation! I've thought about taking off this coming weekend, since the children's school will not be interrupted this way. I wonder whether I should go to my mother's or sister's?"

"I don't think I'd go either place."

"Why not?"

"Because they'll attach too much importance to it, that's why. You'll set the family gossip mill churning. And you have to remember, some of *them* need to know Christ just as Stew needs to. After all, I am assuming you really want your husband converted and able to lead his family, spiritually. The less face-saving he has to do after this minor crisis, the better chance you have for real good to come from it."

"I hadn't thought of it that way," Grace said, softly. "It's true that I don't want to do anything that causes permanent bitterness between us or makes him feel less of a man."

"Right. So if you *do* go away for a couple of days, leave a nice, sweet note behind—not a trace of arrogance. I'd point out that he has come to the place where he is defeating himself—before God, the community, and his family. A brief separation may help him to reevaluate and see how much keeping his family means to him."

"I think I'll do that!" Grace said, with a hopeful lilt in her voice. "And I'll make it clear that this time I'll be back in a couple of days. Only I'll tell him if there's no change on his part, the next time it may be permanent. But where *should* I go?"

"Well, you can come here," I said. "It's a long drive, but it's up to you."

"I'd like that," she said decisively. "And that way, no one else would have to be involved or know what I'm doing."

"Right!" I said. "Bring a sleeping bag for one of the kids; we have beds for the rest of you."

"Great! Expect me sometime Friday night. Now I'd better run and get everything done around here to be ready to go. I want to be sure to leave him his meals for those days."

"By all means. I wouldn't do one thing that gives him the idea you are shirking your role in that family, except for the brief separation from him. And we'll be praying God will get the glory from this whole thing, by bringing Stew to himself. I'll call Dick right away, and ask him if this plan is okay. If you don't hear from me in ten minutes, you'll know he said 'yes.' "

As I hung up, I marveled at the complete change of tone in Grace's voice during that phone call. As I looked out back through our glass doors I noticed our typical Saratoga County bleakness had been banished by sunlight. Trees, still glistening from a recent shower, reached upward in mute praise.

"From grey despair to bright hope! Lord, that's just like You," I whispered. "Now prepare Dick to want to open his home again to people in need. Thank you, God, for such an understanding, good husband."

The weekend was great fun for the children. Dick played ball with all of them, and took them apple picking. Since we live in McIntosh country, our children can hardly wait for fall and these special Saturdays. Grace's children, like ours, ate as fast as they picked that day. But everyone still seemed to have room for hamburgers, after the harvest!

While Dick and the children were at the orchard, Grace and I caught up on several years of visiting. It was easy to see that she needed to talk things out in order to readjust her priorities. She wanted to go home with the right attitude, trusting God to work the changes in Stew and their home that were needed.

We sat on the family room couch folding laundry. Suddenly she picked up a pair of soft, brown mittens and looked at them quizzically.

"What's the matter—need mending?" I asked.

"No, I was just thinking. Some women are like this, Pat. Their 'submission' is the soft, comfy, external part that the husband sees. Underneath is an iron hand, trying to force him and everyone else in the family to do their will."

"What do you mean?" I asked, settling back against the couch. This subject was much more interesting than folding laundry.

"Well, take that gal you and I heard speak on 'Submission to Your Husband's Covering' last year. Not long after her talk, I had a chance to visit her at home when the whole family was there. I noticed that she had certain goals she was determined her husband would meet. So she cloaked her demands in sugar-sweetness of voice, making eyes at him and, in general, using sex as a weapon. I got the feeling they were playing a game. It was her job to make him *think* he was running the show, while she really ran it. I think she rewards him in bed for the goodies she gets out of him at other times."

"Could be," I said, nodding slowly. "I've noticed this idea of using sex as a weapon in a number of books lately, even one best seller. The notion of sex either that way or as a reward for brownie points is totally pagan. There is no way such a distortion of the marital role can be called Biblical. Was there anything else about the gal which struck you as phony?"

"Yes," Grace said, putting down the mittens and picking up a T-shirt. "She said she would not go anywhere or do anything without her husband's 'covering,' quoting a certain Bible teacher who lives nearby. She admires him very much. I have watched her with him on several occasions. I think she really wants to chant his *shibboleths* and be acceptable to him. Unless I miss my signals there, she is flirting with that guy in countless, subtle ways."

"That's a good way to put those words—*shibboleths,*" I mused. "Like the way Jephthah and the men of Gilead spotted the Ephraimites at the fords of Jordan. If they couldn't pronounce the 'sh' they were from the tribe of Ephraim. That's right! That's just the way it is with this new fad of teaching. If you don't call pastors 'shepherds,' authority 'covering,' and being under authority 'submission,' you're not of the 'in-crowd.'

"By the way, what does this Bible teacher's *wife* think of all these shenanigans?"

"Well, I don't know for sure," Grace said, cocking her head to one side as she looked over at me. "But she certainly has been depressed lately. I wonder if she's jealous."

"Who knows?" I said, picking up some socks and getting back to work. "Maybe she had good reason to be. But the shape his wife is in certainly doesn't speak well for his teaching. Pretty rotten fruit, right there in the family."

"That's just like the devil, isn't it?" Grace said. "The ones who make the biggest fuss over something sometimes blow it the worst. What are you going to do with this thing?" She waved a torn T-shirt.

"Throw it in the rag bag," I said, absently tearing it in two after she handed it to me. "That gal we heard teach on 'submission' was like the one Shakespeare talked about: 'Methinks the lady doth protest too much.' "

"Exactly!" Grace squealed. "And the hard knocks these people and their families are getting remind me of Mercutio in *Romeo and Juliet*. Remember how he said of his wound, 'No, 'tis not so deep as a well nor so wide as a church door, but 'tis enough, 'twill serve.' "

I chuckled. Memories of college days came flooding back.

"I'll bet you were an English major, too," I said, reaching for more socks.

"I was," she said, laughing. "Portia was one of my favorite characters, but ol' suicidal Juliet turned my stomach. She was a sap."

"I agree. But you've got to admit the husband in *The Taming of the Shrew* had something! Some women *are* loudmouthed dictators who'd be comfortable with a billy club. It takes a real man to take his place as head in most *any* kind of family, though."

Grace looked out of the window a little wistfully.

"Yes," she said, "and that's the only kind of man any woman really wants or can respect. What disillusions me most about Stew is his wishy-washy, indecisive attitude, especially with the children. He forces me to be the bad guy, the only one with the guts to punish them."

"Then why not communicate that to him when you get back? Why seethe in silence because he won't take his proper role around the house? Just be sure you build him up and back him up when he *does* move in authority. Praising him for discipline of the children should get good results. All of us prefer that to nagging."

Just then the back door burst open and the children tumbled in.

"Mom, Mom!" young Stew called. "Where are you? Did we ever get the *apples* today. And I climbed higher than anybody."

Before Grace had a chance to answer, he had bounded into the family room, his jeans jacket swinging open. Both hands were full of apples.

"Here, have one," he announced, shoving one into Grace's hand.

"I will, but I want to wash it first," Grace said. "Why not give me all those and I'll wash them."

Our older boys plopped into chairs as Grace headed for the kitchen. Beth Ann squatted on the family room rug with Grace's daughter.

"It was really neat, Ma," Beth Ann said, drawing her knees up to her chest. "There was a soft breeze, so we kept from getting hot while we were picking. But it never did get really cold."

"Great!" I said. "How about helping me put away this laundry? Then I'm going to go in and cook hamburgers."

There was a loud expression of approval around the room. Several willing hands grabbed some laundry as a good-will gesture to encourage me to start supper.

"What's for dessert, Ma?" Beth Ann asked, following me to the kitchen.

"Nothing, yet. I do have some ice cream. Wanna make some brownies?"

"Sure!" she said, beaming. "Turn the oven on while I go upstairs to put this stuff away."

Grace turned around at the sink, as she dried the apples.

"It's great the way they help, Pat," she said, handing me a

McIntosh. "Are they always this way?"

"They have to be," I said, matter-of-factly. "Things are just too busy around here to have any of the team not working. Besides, any house I've seen where mother is an unpaid servant never produced the right kind of kids, anyway. Training in the home should be training for *life*—and that involves work, routine and responsibility. I don't think we do them a favor if we don't give them chores and see to it they are done. Remember how both Eli and Samuel failed God in the matter of being proper parents?"

"I think we've been here for more than one reason this weekend," Grace said, wistfully. "Stew thinks I should do everything and that the children should grow up carefree."

"That's disastrous," I said, opening the refrigerator door. "You should tackle that matter right after you get back."

Just then the phone rang. It was the only friend of Grace's who knew where she was.

"Grace," I said. "It's Betty. And she wants to talk to you."

The conversation that followed was mostly one-sided. Grace said little, except that she would be home Sunday night.

"No, don't tell him where I am," she said, finally. "Tomorrow night he'll know, and it sounds to me like his weekend is doing him some good."

After Grace hung up, she joined me at the kitchen counter. By now my hands were deep in ground beef and wheat germ.

"What can I do to help?" she asked.

"How about slicing tomatoes?" I said. "You'll find them in the crisper at the bottom of the refrigerator."

"Where's your cutting board?"

"Here," Beth Ann answered her, reaching for it behind the sugar cannister. She had just come downstairs and was getting things out for baking.

"Billy, come set the table," I called. "Then go down to the cellar and ask Daddy if he can be ready for supper in twenty minutes or so."

Soon the hamburgers sizzled on the griddle, and the smell of brownies wafted through the room. The table was set, and all the young people were in the family room. Johnny had made a fire in the fireplace; we could hear the comforting crackling from the kitchen.

"Pat," Grace said softly. "I couldn't talk in front of the children. But Stew is really upset. Betty says he's been over four times and is more glum than she's ever seen him. And he's not drinking."

"Well, thank God for that," I said. "As we pray, God is working on him."

"The amazing thing about this is the *peace* I feel," Grace said, tapping the tomato knife on the cutting board as she spoke. "Only God could do this for me. Always in the past when he's said, 'Jump,' my immediate response has been, 'How high?' That was bondage."

"You called it," I said. "God never meant for you to be a doormat, if you're a disciple of Jesus. My guess is this change in attitude is going to be your most powerful asset when you get home."

Three months later Stew came to know Jesus Christ in a personal way. There have been ups and downs since then, but Dick and I have no doubt that this couple is going to make it—even in a culture where one out of three marriages ends in divorce. There is love in that home now and, just as important, *respect*. Neither can last very long without the other.

Respect is the climate where love grows toward maturity. Like apple trees, love can survive some cold nights—even improve because of them. It even can make it through severe storms, as long as the *climate* is right. Lots of sunny weather makes for plenty of endurance when the storms come.

So it must be with our families. We can stand arguments and crises as long as the *climate* in the home is good. If there's a basic cheerfulness, optimism, and appreciation for each member of the family, we can stand anything God allows to come our way. But where relationships mildew in the fog of constant discontent and criticism, even a small crisis can be too much.

May the Son of Righteousness, with healing in His wings, shine upon our families, showing us how to love and respect one another. Abiding in His love is basking in the sunshine forever. We won't forget the warmth because of an occasional stormy day!

11 *The Last Beatitude*

As a child I thought the most wonderful gift my parents could give me was a giant ice cream cone. In the Great Depression there was no such thing as a gallon of vanilla or chocolate in the old refrigerator; going out to Roanoke Dairy was a special treat, even though a cone cost only five cents.

In later years Mother and Dad showed their love in different ways. The "no" answer to some of my urgent requests often was my most authentic sign that they still loved me. Oh, I fumed and fussed when they told me I must stay in college that January of my sophomore year. Dad said he did not want a quitter in the family; he would not let me break my mother's heart and leave. I griped and sulked—but stayed. Deep down I knew they were right; there was a quiet assurance in having authority over me at a time like that. Sometimes we cry out for firmness in others because our own rebel hearts would lead us far astray.

Now I realize that that crisis brought a gift of determination from my father to me. That "no" saved me from an aimless, willful course in life. Today I never could win battles with discouragement in front of a typewriter had it not been for times of discipline *then*.

So it is with dealings from our heavenly Father. When we first are born into the family of God, it seems our prayers are answered quickly. Things tend to come easily. Our lives are sheltered by His hand from experiences He later will bring our way.

While we still are babes in Christ, encouragment and praise from fellow Christians are treats like those early ice cream cones. We delight in these things; we thrive on them. But just as

God never intended our bodies to be sustained by an ice cream diet, so He cannot allow us to *depend upon* the praise of men. The staples of spiritual life are made of more solid stuff than soul-pleasing sugar.

Few studies in the Bible bring more rewards from in-depth meditation than the beatitudes. A wealth of light and "living water" emanate from them. Who could fail to recognize that he is richer for being humble, sorry for sin, meek, merciful, pure in heart or a peacemaker? Yet we flinch when we come to Matthew 5:10.

Are you sure they got it right, Lord? we wonder. *Is it blessed, happy, "to be persecuted for righteousness' sake"? Should it not read, "wretched"?*

The Word of God is never wrong. We may not always *like* it, but God's ways and principles are better for us than vegetables, liver, or whole wheat bread. As a child I hated liver, but I eat it now to have a strong body for God's work.

So it is with the last beatitude. Our heavenly Father watches our first steps in the walk of faith carefully. He is there to pick us up when we fall; the milk of the Word is usually there for the drinking. Even the praise of others comes to us as an echo of His approval.

Then slowly things change. The Father loves no less, but sees signs of our growing up. The milk diet, where the Word is fed to us by others, is not as important as solid food. *The meat of the Word we feed ourselves.* Day by day, line upon line, precept upon precept, it builds us up. Only in this way can we mature to the point where we can feed others. Then, as spiritual parents, we gladly give milk to the next generation of babes.

Scripture says "solid food is for the mature, who because of practice have their senses trained to discern good and evil" (Hebrews 5:14). Here is a great clue to God's dealings. Growth in Him is not so much an *age* factor as a *stage* factor. Are we walking in the Spirit? Can we tell the difference between good and evil? If so, it means we have *practiced* what we have read or been taught. We have been doers of the Word, not hearers only. The more we *do,* the more exciting our life, for we find we understand what is really going on around us.

Spiritual warfare will be a natural result of such growth. We shall find that unseen powers of evil operate more often in lives and situations than we dreamed. Thus we begin to take authority over such forces, binding them in the name of Jesus Christ, and loosing people to do the will of God.

Few crises in the life of a believer are so hard to take as *betrayal.* The latter implies intimacy and mutual trust *between friends* over a period of time. The psalmist wrote, "Even my close friend, in whom I trusted, who ate my bread, has lifted up his heel against me" (Psalm 41:9). David experienced betrayal at the hands of Saul, Ahithophel, and his own son, Absalom. Yet the Holy Spirit speaks prophetically here through David concerning Judas, betrayer of the Lord Jesus.

Years ago at Columbia Bible College, Professor Frank Sells told his classes of "the Judas principle." He said one reason why Jesus chose Judas as a disciple was to warn servants of God in every age to expect betrayal within the church. Although the wheat and tares grow together until the harvest, a farmer said one cannot tell the difference *until then.* In the warmest of spiritual circles Satan has his plants. We shall not know for sure about the family identity of everyone in our fellowships until the Lord comes back. But we do have clues, and sometimes final warnings, because of very poor fruit from certain lives. In this way God separates some from us who would destroy us if they could.

The "grain" from tares is so deadly that it can cause convulsions, insanity, or death, if eaten. Thus God's life-saving program of exposing poor fruit becomes vital to a maturing saint. *Jealousy* and *hatred* for the true servant of God is a prime symptom of the phony. In the merciful providence of God He often will allow such sins to surface, however, so that hypocrites intent on destruction of His true servants can be identified.

One day Grace (chapter 10) phoned me in a state of bewildered anguish. The all-wise heavenly Father had seen fit to put her into His "advanced training." Clearly He had given her a gift He reserved for His maturing children, the blessing of betrayal.

"I don't understand what's happening here," she moaned. "Those I was closest to in this area have turned against me and are actively working against the very program we started together for God."

"Praise Jesus," I said. "That's His way of letting you know you are especially beloved of Him: the badge of discipleship."

"But how can you *say* that, Pat?" she asked.

"On the authority of God's Word," I answered. "Jesus said, 'A slave is not greater than his master. If they persecuted Me, they will also persecute you; if they kept My word, they will keep yours also. *But all these things* they will do to you for My name's sake, because they do not know the One who sent Me.'"

"Where is that?" she said, softly.

"John 15:20 and 21. And, by the way, what *did* they do to the Lord Jesus?"

"Crucified Him."

"Yes, and a lot of other unpleasant things besides," I said. "Toward the end of Lord's earthly ministry He had insults, betrayal and unpopularity. Only in the early months was He received well in most places. By the time He faced Calvary He was hated by large numbers, especially the vested interests of the religious community. He's called us to *that* identification with Him as well as to moments of glory and approval."

"But why?" she wailed.

"Because we belong to Him, are associated with His name, and *are being conformed to His image.* Can you imagine what all that means?"

"That we *react* more and more like Him in suffering, I guess," Grace said, the wonder of Him apparent in her voice.

"Yes! The Father is watching, always watching, as He allows the Holy Spirit to mold us and put us through the fires of trial here on earth. It brings great joy to His heart when He sees us learn to function like His Son in life's darkest moments."

"But is there *no other way?*" she whispered, her voice quavering.

"Think of Jesus in Gethsemane," I said. "He asked the same thing. Yet there was no other way but Calvary. *None* of His disciples stuck with Him that night. The Scripture is very terse on this point: "Then all the disciples left Him and fled" (Matthew 26:56).

"But how do you *live through* something like this?"

"You don't," I said, as gently as I could. "We are meant to *die* under such dealings. Remember how He said, 'Unless a grain of wheat falls into the earth and dies, it remains by itself alone; but if it dies, it bears much fruit' (John 12:24). The self-life in us is the hard, exterior shell of the grain. If it dies, God can get much fruit from our lives, afterward."

"But how can you *treat* people who have tried to d . . . d . . . destroy you?" Grace sobbed.

"The same way Jesus did. Pray, 'Father, forgive them; for they do not know what they are doing' (John 23:24). The first Christian martyr prayed like that. Stephen said, as they were stoning him to death, 'Lord, do not hold this sin against them' (Acts 7:60). Our love and acceptance of wrong in the face of malice is the most unmistakable badge of our discipleship."

"Yes, I can see that. Only how does the *truth* ever get heard, when you're being slandered?"

"The Lord will see to that," I answered. "He defends His own in unique ways, and He reserves all vengeance as His prerogative. The truth *will out,* but in His time, not ours. Sometimes the path of ignominy, which results from gossip and malice leveled against us, most furthers His purposes in our lives. We learn the quiet walk of faith and absolute trust in *Him,* rather than dependence on praise from man.

"In these experiences He builds a hidden strength in us, like iron. Then when hard times come, we are amazed to find a calm joy in ourselves that many lack. Make no mistake about it, difficult days are coming for the church of the living God. When they do, there must be those whose souls are iron-clad as well as love-warmed. Be glad for the training now!"

The crying had subsided.

"Pat, how do you know these things?" she asked, very quietly.

"The only way most of us learn anything," I answered matter-of-factly. "By experience—God's 'jungle camp.' Once the Lord took me from a 'ring of enemies.' That was the phrase He gave me as I prayed for light and understanding. No trial was ever rougher; no other has ever brought such dividends."

"Were they very close friends?"

"I thought them so. But God did a surprising thing when He

separated us. He seemed to push me out of the their range of attack. He put me in a new situation with a different emphasis of ministry, and set me on a whole new course for writing and speaking."

"What *is* the new emphasis?" Grace asked.

"The Christian's obligation to be *salt* and *light* in our nation: to repent of our sins of indifference, neglect and pride that let the nation be taken over by the devil; then to pitch in, roll up our shirtsleeves, and win it back for God."

"I see. Does that include politics?"

"Yes, I think politics will have to be out in front of the concerns the Lord is giving His people these days, because government affects all of our lives and His work. A dangerous nucleus of militant radicals who derive supernatural help from the pit are trying to capture our country for Satan. God is looking for Christians who care enough about Him and His Word to get into this battle and fight for righteousness."

"What are examples of radical activity?" Grace asked, sounding amazed.

"Attempts to force the FCC to stop religious broadcasting. Rewriting of American history to remove our godly heritage from whole generations. Textbook slanting which elevates evil and ridicules righteousness. It's a big topic—would take us *hours* to discuss. Better wait until I see you next for that."

"I agree," Grace said. "But tell me, do you think God is trying to get *me* out of the range of my enemies, too? Could He be redirecting my whole life as He has yours?"

"Could be," I said, looking out the window at the drifted snow blowing about in the yard. "Sometimes when the winds of change blow through our lives we are confused while we are in the storm as to what God is doing. But he makes it clear in time. And He *protects* us and *provides for* us through whatever situation He puts us in. Whether *in* the lions' den with the mouths of the lions sealed, or in a place far from the lions, God chooses our way for us. And He does it according to that which brings Him the most glory."

"I'm sure you're right there, Pat," Grace said, "But I'm puzzled about something else. These knotty situations with people on 'the inner circle' often mean a total break in relationship. Yet isn't God's will *always* forgiveness and reconciliation?"

"Forgiveness, yes; reconciliation, no," I said. "Paul wrote Titus to 'reject a *factious man* after a first and second warning, knowing that such a man is perverted and is sinning, being self-condemned' (Titus 3:10,11). Proverbs 6:19 mentions 'one who spreads strife among brothers' as one of the seven things the Lord hates. When you run into this problem among Christians, and there is no repentance from it, surgery of the sick member is inevitable. Otherwise the cancer will spread to the rest of the Body of Christ. That's why Matthew 5:21-26 and 18:15-17 are in the Word. They tell us how to handle severe problems in relationships."

Grace was silent for a minute. Then she spoke, an electric quality to her voice. She sounded more like she was thinking aloud than talking to me.

"Why, this must be the other side of the coin. I think the Lord is just wanting me to go on with Him, regardless of the opposition of certain people, and they were standing in His way! Yet I've been thinking He *had* to want us all together. I thought I'd failed because I couldn't change their minds. Now I see it. *God* wants them out to keep them from ruining His work."

"Sure sounds that way," I commented. "Even the apostle Paul had that problem. He wrote Timothy that Demas, 'having loved this present world' (II Timothy 4:10), had deserted him. In the same letter he mentioned that Alexander the coppersmith had done him much harm. But then he concluded with that all-important principle of dealing with troublemakers: 'the Lord will repay him according to his deeds.' Forgive, regardless of *what* happens. But shut out any thought of vengeance or retribution; that all belongs to God."

After we hung up, I came back to my desk and opened my Bible to the last beatitude, Matthew 5:10-12.

"Blessed are those who have been persecuted for the sake of righteousness, for theirs is the kingdom of heaven. Blessed are you when men revile you, and persecute you, and say all kinds of evil against you falsely, on account of Me. Rejoice, and be glad, for your reward in heaven is great, for so they persecuted the prophets who were before you."

Outside it was snowing again, not just drifting. It was the fourth storm of the week. Our lawn lay under a heavy blanket of merciful white—merciful, because it covered such chaotic ruin. Our devastated grass was entombed between the snow and frozen earth. Yet we knew we faced a big job come spring, putting in a new lawn on that formidable bank.

Last spring Billy, our youngest, had warned us that something was wrong. Yet somehow we had never taken his comments seriously enough to really look.

"Mommy... Daddy..." he said more than once. "There are little holes out there in the lawn; go and see."

But we never went. So the grubs ate, multiplied and fulfilled the many functions of their life cycle on their way to becoming Japanese beetles, unhindered by us. Thus by midsummer (when all grubs worthy of the name go underground) they destroyed the roots of the grass they used for shelter. Heartlessly they ate and ate, while Dick watered more each day, wondering why the lawn didn't pick up!

Our only hope was for a new lawn, a new beginning.

So it is with certain relationships or even with works for God that all of us once knew. When the enemies have done their work, no amount of watering dead relationships will bring them back to life. We have to deal with the enemies; then clear away the debris. Only afterward are we ready for a fresh start, for new direction.

Grace was facing what I had faced in my own life: the death of old programs, old relationships. She would have to clear away the debris from her thinking: forgive those who had wronged her, and put away all resentment forever. Only then could she see clearly to sow new seed on cleansed soil, and experience God's springtime.

My brother once said that God's death-resurrection theme is repeated every year with fall and winter followed by spring. I like that. All of nature preaches the Gospel every year in a temperate climate.

God's will for us is a balanced life, dwelling in His Word and

His presence. It brings a markedly temperate climate. The fruit of the Spirit that the King James Bible calls "temperance" is translated by contemporary scholars as "self-control." The Lord is pleased when we are not so rocked by betrayal that we give in to bitterness and resentment; He rejoices when we go the whole way with Him and rejoice, ourselves.

Our heavenly Father no more wants "quitters" in the family than my earthly father did, when I was eighteen years old. The blessing of betrayal tests us, so that He can find out for sure what stuff we are made of.

Are we content to lose earthly friends and even Christian fellowship, as long as we abide in Him? Or do we hang on dearly to the past, as did Lot's wife?

And are we willing to be glad, just because He says so, when our lives run counter to what we would have planned for ourselves?

How we answer these questions may well determine whether we ever shall be able to obey our Lord's command, "Therefore you are to be perfect (mature), as your heavenly Father is perfect" (Matthew 5:48).

12 *Some Awesome Visions*

Last Mother's Day, Pastor had several women speak during the evening service. Each of us had spent roughly a quarter of a century raising families—some more, some less. Each could rejoice in grown children in whom God was working.

It was a thrilling evening. A warm glow seemed to rest on our whole congregation as we shared testimonies of God's faithfulness as we brought up our children for Him. Many women jumped to their feet to give God the glory for victory in their homes before three of us spoke from the pulpit.

Eileen Thornton, whose warm smile and thoughtful concern have uplifted many in our church, was the first to speak. Her dynamic husband and sons, as zealous for the Lord as they are courteous and dependable, adorn her life as no words could. Clothed in the peace so characteristic of her, she taught on *consistency* and *balance* in raising children. I sat there drinking it in, praying that God would work these secrets into my own life.

Next it was my turn to speak on *discipline*. It was heartwarming to see the grins on Beth Ann and Billy as I told of our many trips to the first floor den and the "rod" that is kept there. No bitterness seemed to rise up at the mention of "the board of education applied to the seat of learning." My heart welled up in thankfulness to God for such children, to whom regular chores are a way of life, just as memorizing Scripture is. As I thought of Charlie and Johnny away at college, whom God is molding for His purposes, I was glad Dick and I had chosen the narrow way. Now they have chosen it for themselves, and are learning to walk in it.

Then Win Bloxom spoke. A soft-spoken, radiant dynamo, she shared how God had brought both beautiful daughters of theirs to His choice of marriages. Although each had nearly married a "Mr. Wrong," God had heard Win and Bob's prayers and had moved in to change things.

One of her stories particularly struck me. At a certain point, their fun-loving Janie met a young man who shared Jesus with her. He was not a committed Christian and was experimenting with drugs. Yet Janie, through encounters with other believers and Young Life, came to know Jesus Christ as her personal Lord and Savior. She continued seeing this boy, encouraging him to change his way of life. However, instead of becoming a new creature himself, he tried to pull her into his realm. She seemed caught in a web spun from her own compassion.

Finally Janie announced to her parents that she and the young man had made marriage plans, and mentioned the date that she had set. Smiling sweetly, Win announced that she and Bob already had vacation plans for the week and could not be present. Of course, the young people were free to do as they wished!

Only parents who have learned *the secret of intercession* can know what trust in the Lord is inherent in such a reaction to life's great crises. Bob and Win realized they could not *order* Janie to change her plans; but they had faith that the One to whom they had committed her *could!*

This tactic deflated any aura of romance in their daughter. Somehow her marriage plans fizzled with the prospect of no parental attendance at the wedding. Even worse, there were no angry words or stern pronouncements to rebel against!

Not long afterward Janie and the young man broke up. Then she yielded any idea of marriage to the Lord, content now to "seek first His kingdom, and His righteousness" (Matthew 6:33). Soon she met Bruce, who put God first in his life. They were drawn together through caring for a woman who was dying of cancer. A few months later they were married—with the blessing of the Lord and their parents!

As I listened to this testimony, Win's wisdom astonished me. I wondered if I could have "kept my cool" in a crisis like that, and I asked God to make a way for me to get better acquainted with Win. He answered by allowing Dick and me a vacation with the Bloxoms. In July 1974 we went to a Christian Life

Conference in New Wilmington, Pennsylvania. It was one of the best weeks Dick and I ever remember.

On the long drives to and from the conference, the men did all the driving, having a great time talking together in the front seat of the Bloxoms' car. Win and I, in the back seat, also had many hours sharing. Since our lives are usually too busy for such times at home, this was a special "extra" for all of us from a loving heavenly Father. He knows His children sometimes need an opportunity to talk with others of like mind.

"Win," I said, on the way back from the conference, "with life as brutal as it is, sometimes, you could not *always* have been the way you are now. Your calm and compassion, that reservoir of energy—when did these things *bloom* in your life?"

"When I met the Lord Jesus Christ and learned to yield to His Spirit," she said, quietly. "Not too many years ago I lay beside our swimming pool in Phoenix and debated whether or not I should just roll off and drown. I saw no reason to go on."

"Why? Had you gone through some great trial?"

"Well, a number of smaller ones, perhaps. Like the Chinese torture of the steady drip of a faucet, they had taken their toll. We moved to Phoenix in July 1961. The heat was terrible, and I always have suffered in hot weather. Since we had come from a New Mexico altitude of 6500 feet, the change was especially hard.

"Then, to make things worse, we had to stay for six weeks in a motel where the air conditioning had broken down. We bought a house which needed extensive repair, and I found myself painting—alone—while Bob was away on a business trip. The parade of plumbers and sub-contractors seemed endless, and money was scarce. Every penny had to go into the house.

"In 1962 our home was robbed while we were away. Later that year I was also held up at gunpoint at the office where I worked part-time. Each of these shocks seemed to leave me with less and less reserve strength. I loved Bob and he loved me, but we could not seem to help each other. We went to a counselor at church and a professional counselor as well. Both told us there was nothing wrong with either of us, or with our marriage. I realize now we just needed Jesus."

"Did you find Him right after this counseling?" I asked, fascinated that God seems to use this "jungle camp" method of hard experience in each life He uses.

"No, I wasn't at the very bottom yet," Win said, laughing, as she looked over at me. "We went into a construction phase again at home, putting in the pool. Then I endured six months of agony with an ear infection—improperly diagnosed until Bob took me to a specialist. The near-suicide happened toward the end of that period. Yet—now that I've read your books—I realize *both the infection and the depression came after submitting to hypnosis!* At a dinner meeting with Bob, a guest hypnotist chose me as his subject. We knew no Scripture then and did not know this was wrong."

"Wow!" I said. "It's something, the risks we take through sheer ignorance. Did you meet the Lord *after* the pool incident?"

"No, just before." Win folded her sweater on her lap and looked down. "I think the enemy fooled me that it would make no difference what I did then, since I was ready for heaven. A few weeks before that, Bob's boss and his wife had invited us to a Faith-at-Work Conference. We were thrilled with the reality there. We both came to Christ when the invitation was given, and prayed at once for some continuing fellowship. Right afterward we met a young couple who also were praying for Christian friends! That began a Bible study and prayer group which lasted for five years, until they moved away."

"Praise Jesus," I said, grinning. "God always puts us in Bible school, doesn't He? With Paul it was alone with Him in Arabia. With us it was a Long Hill Chapel in New Jersey, and Columbia Bible College. But He always gets His children into His Word. Babies without any milk would be in pretty sad shape. Was it this study that brought you out of your depression?"

"Partly," Win said reflectingly as she gazed out at the hilly countryside. "But much of that had to do with discovering a *purpose* for my life. I often had dreamed of having my own secretarial business. In 1968 a friend and I went into partnership. Our daughters were teenagers; one was already in college. The business went well and the money helped put both girls through school."

"Wonderful!" I said. "My mother did that for me and my brother: worked to help put us through college. Once I asked her how I could pay her back, and she said, 'It's a debt you pay to your own children when they are grown.' She was right.

"I told the Lord I would be full-time in His work, if He would take full responsibility for educating our children. He's surely been faithful. Johnny has a full scholarship to the Coast Guard Academy, and Charlie has a Regents Scholarship which helps a lot. Somehow the money's always there to pay the rest of his Nyack bill. We have no college debts. But I bet you ran into some narrow-minded Christians who never thought about college costs and just judged you for having a business, didn't you?"

"Oh, of course," Win said, laughing. "But when you're following the Lord and have your eyes on Him, you really don't care that much what other people say or think. I was absolutely certain I was in the will of God in that venture. He kept blessing it every step of the way, as Joshua 1 and Psalm 1 both promise. I am convinced that *many Christian women are suffering from a need to achieve:* to put all the talents God has given them to work. I found in the busy world of business a fertile field for witness. I could speak for Jesus Christ many times. We tried to do the best possible job which could be found anywhere in Phoenix. Before long we had three offices and several secretaries working for us."

"And to think you work as a *volunteer* secretary in our church," I said, shaking my head. "Have you ever been restless to get back into the business world?"

"No," Win said, thoughtfully. "I had deep assurance before we moved here that God was going to set me into His full-time service and that I probably would not be making money. That first Sunday at Pineview, when Pastor said his secretary was on vacation and he needed help in the office, I *knew.* I just said in prayer, 'Thank You, Lord. I hear Your voice.' And of course I never got out of the office with two new assistant pastors coming, the bookstore opening, and all the wonderful things God has been doing at Pineview."

About three hours later we were driving through the mountains near Oneonta. Both Win and I saw the moon rising over one of the peaks. We each gave a startled "Oh!" before it disappeared behind the trees.

"Did you see what I saw?" I whispered to Win, wondering if I had gone mad.

"If you saw the moon ringed with blood, then the answer is 'yes,' " she said, quietly.

"Yes!" I said, out loud this time. "Just like a moon a child would draw, with a heavy crayon line of bright red all around it."

"What's going on back there?" Dick broke in. He was driving, and neither he nor Bob had been looking up toward the mountains.

"Then you didn't see the moon with that red ring around it?" I asked.

"You mean like a harvest moon?" Bob offered. "No, we didn't see it."

"No, not like that, Bob," Win said excitedly, leaning over toward him and putting a hand on his shoulder. "It had a bright red ribbon of color around it."

"The Bible speaks of the moon being turned into blood as one of the key signs of the end times," I said.

By now all four of us were eagerly watching for the moon to appear again. We all settled back with sighs of disappointment when it did. This time it looked like it always does.

"How do you account for the way you saw it before?" Dick asked, always of a practical turn of mind.

"I don't know," I said, "but I think it must have been a vision, the blood-ring around it. Whatever it was is not on it now."

"And I believe we *both* were allowed to see it so that we could not talk ourselves out of it later," Win added.

For an hour or so after that, the four of us had a lively talk about what God must have wanted to impress upon us. But we never came up with any real answers.

Recently I asked Win to have lunch with me to share any insights we might have received about that vision in the six months since our trip. As we settled into the platform rockers on either side of our family room fireplace, it occurred to me that we had not had time for a real chat since our vacation.

"Win," I asked her, "what do you think God was trying to say to us that evening we saw the moon encircled in blood?"

"That the church will be on earth during the time of earth's great trial," she said softly, "and that we shall be kept as completely as the moon was within that ring of blood."

"That's fascinating," I said. "And it ties in with a thought I have had for some time about 'the days of Noah.' Remember how we are told that the time of the coming of the Son of Man will be *just like* those days? Well Noah was kept *on the earth,* but in a place of refuge, while the world around him was being judged."

"That's right, isn't it?" Win said, smiling, and cocking her head slightly to one side. "What about you? Have any other ideas about that vision?"

"Well," I said, "my main impression is that God wants us to know that the fiercest kinds of times are coming. As I searched the Scriptures when we got back, I discovered that both Joel 2:31 and Revelation 6:13 state that the *whole* moon will become like blood. It seems to me that the Lord is telling us we are on the periphery of the time of blood. The day will come when God shall reveal the devastated condition of the earth after one-fourth of its population has died—perhaps by such a spectacular sign in the heavens as that blood-red moon. Only then the moon will be *drenched* in blood—and I think everyone on earth will see it."

"That's interesting," Win said. "And I've been wondering often, lately, whether some of the other things God has shown me are related to these end-times prophecies, as well."

"Have you had *other* visions, then?" I asked, a sense of awe settling over me.

"Yes," she said quietly. "One of them has been given to me twice. It's a vast mound: a convex thing, bleak grey, with huge crevasses in it. In the first vision like that, I saw the shadow of the Lord's form above it. He had His hands lovingly outstretched as if to assure His people and give them confidence that He will be with us. Through the fiery trials we are to keep our hearts and minds stayed on Him."

"That mound," I interrupted. "Oh Win, I think that's the earth after nuclear war."

"It could be," she said. "That's the part of the vision I saw again a second time: this time just the grey mound with crevasses, but followed by a second scene of flat plains with withered stubble on them rather than crops."

"That could be the fields after such a war." I winced. "Or even a separate condition of famine just shown as a distinct trial. After all, Revelation 6, which lists these calamities in order, introduces the red horse of war first. The black horse of famine follows, where a quart of wheat sells for a day's wage. Your visions strongly confirm the sense of urgency I have had since we both saw that blood-ring around the moon. I believe God is seeking to prepare us for momentous times."

"I'm sure of it," Win said, quietly. "But the strangest thing about all this is that I'm *not afraid;* just looking forward to it with an inner expectancy I can neither explain nor ignore. Aren't you thrilled that God chose us to live in His last generation?"

"Yes!" I said, jumping up and going to the picture window. Overhead the sky was grey but getting lighter than when we had come into the family room. "Sometimes I feel like shouting! There's such a sense of expectancy on the inside. And the God of Daniel can still keep His own safe in the lions' den; He can still deliver from the fiery furnace all those who stay true to Him! Somehow I think the self-same experiences that will bring annihilation to the Lord's enemies are going to mean transformation, for us. I believe there may be more miracles in these last days than in all the stretches of time up to this point. And the plains you saw will not *always* be covered with stubble."

"Surely not," Win agreed. "But what do you have in mind?"

"A dream I had when I was eleven years old," I said, still looking up at the sky and remembering that night as if it were yesterday.

"I stood on a plain with many people, all looking up at the night sky studded with stars. Then suddenly the stars were blacked out for a huge area, stretching from one end of the horizon to the other, and high into the heavens. The thing that obscured the stars had a definite shape, like a castle, and it came into view as we all stared. Like waterfalls of diamonds it shimmered there, as it appeared—a huge city with shining pathways surrounding its outer walls. On them stood millions of angels or saints, and they all were singing as they came into view. I shall never forget the sound of that music; nothing on earth has ever been like it."

My voice choked up and I could feel the tears slipping down my cheeks as they always do when I speak of that dream.

"Was that all?" Win asked, after a brief pause.

"No," I said. "At the top of the castle or city a huge scroll was stretched across. And as we stood there watching, an unseen Hand wrote three words in script on it, in letters that must have been miles high. It wasn't said the way you and I would say it. That's probably why I have never been able to forget those three words: *He is come.*"

"Could that be the sign of the Son of Man which the Lord Jesus speaks of in the Olivet discourse?" Win asked.

"Perhaps. Who knows?" I whispered. "But when I saw it I did not know Him nor know He was coming back. Yet that experience held me through the wasteland of college agnosticism and brought me back again and again to the fact that there is a God who loves us enough to reveal Himself to us. And after my conversion, when I got into the Word, I discovered the new Jerusalem of Revelation 21—a city half as big as the United States and as high as wide, coming down out of heaven from God. No matter what kind of destruction man brings on himself and this planet because of sin, we have that to look forward to. And *then* there shall be no more crying or mourning or pain . . ."

13 *Deborah? or Jezebel?*

Today's mail brought an encouragment from the Father like a quick hug from an earthly loved one.

Char Potterbaum, author of *If You See Lennie,* started her note to me like this: "It seems that everywhere I've gone, you've warmed the bed previously." Although we have never met, Char empathizes with me because we both have writing and teaching ministries. Further along in her letter she wrote, "So often I have gotten the hint that 'it-would-be-best-if-your-husband-traveled-with-you,' etc. But no one seems to know just how the extra flight ticket is going to be paid, and just how his own work is going to continue.... Wish I had time to fire a lot of questions your way—like, what is your pastor's response to your ministry?" (See the forward of this book for his answer to that one!)

Char, like me, is a wife and mother. She has doubtless been criticized, as I have, for being God's servant. Since we live in an age when the whole question of women's ministry is under fire, an ostrich approach to it will never do. Those of us whom the Lord has called for His work must know we are in His will and be serene in it, regardless of persecution. Then we can be "ready to give an answer" to those who wonder how such a thing can be.

Once I had the privilege of praying with a certain man of God. At that time I had a health problem; my own purpose in seeking prayer was to ascertain whether I should have surgery or not. God's servant suggested we both pray in the Spirit (i.e. in the prayer language), which we did. Then he got an interpretation, which was repeated twice: "This is My servant; I will get glory from her life."

At the time, I was somewhat perplexed, for I felt my prayer

had not been answered. I went ahead and had the surgery, which proved minor. Several years later the man who had prayed with me began challenging a woman's right to teach the Word. Thus I have come to see that the interpretation of the prayer language that day was not for me, but for him. The sovereign God looked down the corridor of time and saw the morass of legalism into which His servant was heading. Clearly He was warning the man and endorsing my ministry.

One wonders whether Deborah, judge of Israel and wife of Lappidoth, ever faced critics. She broke many modern rules which man has set up! She did not minister with her husband, but sat "under the palm tree of Deborah" (Judges 4:5), which sounds like a private office to me. Some would say she went into battle without "covering" since her husband was home or elsewhere, apparently, while she served the Lord in this way.

But Deborah had wisdom, and "the sons of Israel *came up to her* for judgment" (Judges 4:5). That quality comes only from the fear of God, and is somewhat scarce in any age. No wonder people are willing to go to great lengths to get it.

Probably Deborah never faced young seminary students, as I have, with their Bibles open to I Timothy 2:12! Such experiences have sharpened my sense of humor, and I am convinced they are encounters planned by God for the young legalists who initiate them. The Lord is seeking to find out if we will learn His *ways,* as Moses did, or be forever fixated upon His *acts,* as the children of Israel were (Psalm 103:7).

God cannot contradict Himself. Since I Timothy 2:12 *appears* to counter other teaching on women, even Paul's, I have been intrigued that the Holy Spirit saw to it that the apostle Paul included the word "I" in that verse. A Midwest pastor understood this well, for he introduced me on the last night of a teaching conference in this way:

"I'm glad my name is not the apostle Paul," he said, "for if it were, I would not suffer a woman to teach!"

Since Paul himself *commanded* women to teach other women in Titus 2:3-5, and mentions many female Roman names as "servants of the Lord" in Romans 16, what *did* he mean in the controversial verse on which many are basing so much doctrine these days?

Gerald Derstine wrote in *Women's Place in the Church* that this passage does not refer to the devotional teaching of the Word at all. He sees it as a warning to the young pastor never to allow himself to be dominated by matriarchal figures within in the church. Most pastors face this problem and must stand their ground, maintaining their authority over such individuals. A congregation can be utterly destroyed by some wealthy shrew who controls it through using the pastor as a wind-up toy.

Yet how devastating it is to apply this passage to women opening the Word under the anointing of the Holy Spirit, at the request of their pastors and elders and under their authority. Loren Cunningham, director of Youth with a Mission, also recently has affirmed the right of women to teach and minister. So have Kenneth Hagin, Dennis Bennett, and many others.

Rita Bennett has an excellent section on this matter in her book, *I'm Glad You Asked That*. She summarizes her argument: "If a married woman is submitted to her husband and to her pastor, and *they want her to teach* in a Bible class composed of men and women, I believe the Scripture supports her in doing so."

Rita and I agree. We had a conversation about this when we were both speakers at the Greater Pittsburgh Charismatic Conference. Quite a few of us see the current furor over women's ministry arising out of man's basic rebellion toward God. How often we mortals try to confine God to a box!

The book of Galatians was written because those believers had fallen into a vicious trap of legalism. Instead of walking in the Spirit, the Lord's people were trying to reduce His ways to a few rules. Paul warned that this was *another gospel* and could not be tolerated.

God always deals with the *heart;* He watches the *motives* for our acts. Current teaching on "submission" and "the woman's place" must be kept in His balance. *Men who are walking in the Spirit, speaking the truth in love, are not threatened by a woman's ministry;* men plagued by insecurity may be. All of us must realize that Psalm 105:15 applies to women as well as men; we need to have a holy caution about "touching God's anointed."

For some time many women prominent in ministry were single: Kathryn Kuhlman, Gladys Aylward, Basilea Schlink, Corrie ten Boom. But lately several married women are being used more and more of God: Vicki Jamison, Rita Bennett, Jean Darnell of England, Major Kay Huber Roberts, Joy Dawson of New Zealand.

I will never forget the privilege of hearing Joy Dawson speak in Dallas last year, the only night I had free from speaking engagements. Just before her message—one of the last of a series—a student at Christ for the Nations came up and confessed his sin of resenting her coming; his feeling that she, as a woman, had no right to teach. Then he admitted that the Lord had broken him more under her ministry than ever before!

Such are the ways of a soveriegn God. Could it be that He still exercises His right to choose Deborahs as well as Daniels? Did He not promise (Joel 2:29), "And even *on the male and female servants I will pour out My spirit* in those days"?

Do spiritual blinders keep some from realizing what God is doing in these last days? In the final analysis, *does He need their approval?*

I think not. When I came to this realization, the Lord set me free from a need for human approval. As long as my own husband and pastor approve of the ministry God has given me, I am under authority and therefore "covered" to do whatever God calls me to do. "If therefore the Son shall make you free, you shall be free indeed" (John 8:36).

Dorothy Buchanan, an Aglow president in Dayton, Ohio, shared how God showed her the incredible freedom He has for His daughters. In a dream, she was taken through a beautiful old farm house with many rooms, each one brightly decorated. As she went from room to room she clapped her hands, catching her breath for sheer joy. Soon she heard, "This is your role as My feminine servant; and there is much more outside."

Then she ran outdoors, breathless with wonder at all the loveliness: gardens, fields and meadows as far as the eye could see.

When she awakened there was a holy awe and love for the

Lord in her that surpassed anything she had known before.

"Pat," she told me that fall day in 1974, "I'm convinced that's why Satan so desperately fights our finding our true role as women. He plans counterfeits such as 'women's lib' and 'doormat submission' hoping desperately we'll buy one of the lies and never come into that glorious freedom."

"You've really struck gold in that idea," I said, my eyes filling up. "No one in her right mind would spurn the sparkling life you have in Christ for the drab despair I have seen in some women. A negative self-image is the number one problem of women in America today. Yet those living out a self-fulfilling prophecy of unworthiness-to-serve have a shock coming at the judgment seat of Christ. There they will discover that God never intended such a life for them, nor will He reward them for following false teaching."

"But what is to be done to convince them otherwise?" she asked, eyes wide.

"Tell them the truth," I said, "and live it before them. We should be *salt* to make them thirsty; *then* free channels of the Lord's living water bubbling up from within. They must see it is not enough to have one's *own* thirst quenched. We are to be channels of living water as our lives are given totally to the Lord for service to others."

"Pat, there's a lot of confusion in this area over these things. We've had quite a bit of wrong teaching or emphasis. I wish you could teach on women's ministry before you leave."

"I intend to. Tonight. At the Maynard's prayer meeting where I am to speak."

Actually, I was not sure of my subject until that moment. But a message had been brewing in my mind for weeks on "Deborah? Or Jezebel?" This seemed the right time and place to give it.

My message that night began with God's warning to the church at Thyatira: "But I have this against you, that you tolerate the woman Jezebel, *who calls herself a prophetess,* and she teaches and leads my bond-servants astray, so that they commit acts of immorality and eat things sacrificed to idols. And I gave her time to repent; and she does not want to repent of her immorality" (Revelation 2:20, 21).

The fruit of this woman's ministry was rotten: it produced immorality and occultism among God's people. So today there are satanic "plants" in Christian groups who are leading astray the gullible. We turned to the Old Testament to see the Jezebel character fully developed, so that we might learn to recognize it.

First, Jezebel was a Baal-worshiper; she had the wrong god.

Second, she worked indirectly through a weak man, her husband, King Ahab. Using him like the proverbial wind-up toy, she perpetrated incredible slander, malice and murder under a heavy veneer of religious talk. When Naboth refused to sell his vineyard to her husband, she got it for him. Her method? "Proclaim a fast, and seat two worthless men before him, and let them testify against him, saying, 'You cursed God and the king.' Then take him out and stone him to death" (I Kings 21: 9,10).

Third, Jezebel hated God's true prophet. After God sent the fire down on Mount Carmel to consume Elijah's sacrifice, and he killed the 400 prophets of Baal, Jezebel determined to kill Elijah. The very next day God's anointed servant lay under a juniper tree so depressed he wanted to die, for fear of Jezebel! We should never underestimate either the demonic or soul power released through such a woman.

Fourth, Jezebel's craven ambition destroyed her femininity; she reminds us of Lady Macbeth, who cried, "unsex me," in order to have the frame of mind for murder. Without a gentle sweetness from within, no one has a right to call herself a woman. Jezebel, having lost that, tried to cover up her hardness with paint and even seduce her assassin, so total was her deception at the end (II Kings 9:30 ff.).

The final end of a contemporary Jezebel will be no less severe. Indeed, we know she will spend eternity in hell if she refuses to repent. Let us not fall into the trap of the "sloppy agape" of Thyatira and tolerate such fiendism. We must go and warn such women of their deception. Follow the pattern of Matthew 18:15-17. Where an individual hears us, we may well have saved a soul from death (James 5:20); even where she does not, the rest of the body of Christ can be saved from the destruction caused by the spread of her spiritual cancer.

But what of Deborah? Does she differ from the *phony* female servant? Yes, in every way.

First, *God* called her a prophetess (Judges 4:4). She did not proclaim herself one. The Lord put His unmistakable stamp on His servant, and brought such good fruit from her ministry that there was no doubt as to its origin.

Second, she was "the wife of Lappidoth," which I take to mean her life was "in divine order." She did not have to work furtively behind her husband, either pushing him or using him, but had a ministry in her own right.

Third, the gift of wisdom was so marked in her life that *people came to her.* She heard from God, and strong men recognized this to be so. Barak was a general: certainly nobody's weakling or puppet. God had been training him for the great test against Sisera's army; yet he was humble enough to want God's anointed servant on hand. Incidentally, my guess is that Deborah was very feminine. Experience teaches us that strong men despise masculine, dominating women.

Fourth, Deborah had the ability to "tell it like it is," the ungarnished truth. She never stooped to deception or religious pretense. When she informed Barak that Sisera would be vanquished by a woman (Jael), Barak probably was less than overjoyed. Yet he knew Deborah spoke for God, and he was not guilty of condemning God's anointed.

In Judges 5 the Holy Spirit shows us the heart of this amazing woman whom He used to save a nation: She gave the glory to God and blessed Him for victory in the warfare (verses 2 and 3); she saw the primary need of her time, i.e., "the highways were deserted and travelers went by roundabout ways" (verse 6); occultism had taken over and God's people were not prepared for battle (verse 8); she had a heart of compassion for both leaders and people to be in God's will (verses 2 and 9); and she called her people to *right action* and *true worship* (the rest of the chapter).

In concluding this message, I gave a few simple questions which can be used to test any female ministry:

1. Is she *under authority?*
2. Is she *feminine?*
3. Is she *humble,* or does arrogance come through?

4. Is she *truthful,* no matter what the cost?
5. What is the *fruit* of her ministry? We should be able to look at the lives of her earthly and spiritual children and see the fruit of the Spirit, as well as in herself.

One such woman is Rita Warren of Brockton, Massachusetts. A dynamic witness for Jesus Christ, this Italian-American immigrant does not know the meaning of the word "no" if it comes from those who oppose God's Word. Once when her daughter was severely ill, she made a covenant with the Lord: "God, you heal my daughter and I get prayer back into the schools of Massachusetts."

The whole story is told in her recently published book, *Mom, They Won't Let Me Pray,* written with Dick Schneider of *Guideposts.* However, the facts speak for themselves. God honors His Word in the lives of those who trust Him by acting on it. He healed Rita's daughter, and July 23, 1973, students in Brockton stood for "one minute of silence for meditation or prayer." For the first time since the Supreme Court decision banning school prayer, time was set aside for God in Massachusetts schools, by a new state law.

Since that victory Rita has not been idle. She plans to take her fight to get prayer back into *all* United States schools all the way to the Supreme Court. She has debated on television with Madalyn Murray O'Hair, who has become a personal friend. She prays that the well-known atheist will see God's love in her.

In 1974, when the Massachusetts State Legislature was debating a bill against pornography, Rita sat in the balcony. While the lawmakers had their discussions, she was busy cutting lurid pictures from pornographic magazines available on any newsstand. When they voted to table the bill, she jumped to her feet, shouting down at them:

"You down there! You have been fighting this obscenity bill for three weeks. If this is what you want, here—have it! Tell your children that their daddy is a dirty old man!"

With that, she threw down her handiwork. As the hundreds of obscene pictures wafted down on the desks (and heads) of the legislators, a strange thing happened. A great awe settled over the men. Some blew their noses furiously. Before long a roll-call vote on the filth issue was taken, and *that day* an anti-obscenity law was passed in Massachusetts.

It is no accident that God is raising up modern Deborahs at this crucial point in our nation's history. It has long been said that "she who rocks the cradle rules the nation." Mothers who see the great spiritual issues of our time can be mightily used of God to turn this generation back to Him. Our nation has sunk so low into moral filth and ruin that it may be too late, as it was in Jeremiah's days, to *prevent* judgment. Still, there *must* be those who will speak out for God *before, during* and *after* judgment.

In the fall of 1974 I interviewed Barbara Keating during her race for the U.S. Senate against Jacob Javits and Ramsey Clark. A Vietnam war widow with five children, she had been drafted by the Conservative Party to run a race she could not hope to win. She agreed, in order to have the opportunity to speak out openly for righteousness in government.

Pert and petite, she looked more like a tiny version of Princess Grace than a politician. An active Catholic, she expressed her faith in God somewhat differently than I would mine. But I knew her to be a daughter of the King when I asked her, "Were you embittered at the time your husband was killed?"

"No," she answered, looking at me thoughtfully. "I was strengthened by his death rather than destroyed by it."

"Do you think our nation's straying from God has any bearing on our present situation?"

"Absolutely," she said. "Loss of faith in God has put this country in a position of defeat."

Better rather than bitter, Barbara as a young widow had thrown her energies and time into projects which would help turn back the tide of evil in the society her children must grow up in. Not a hand-wringer but a doer, she fearlessly exposed leftist radical activity in public schools. One letter she wrote to a local editor exposing teachers who drove students to picket at draft offices ended up as a front-page feature article.

I followed her activities with great admiration throughout the campaign. At election time she only got fifteen percent of the vote, but it represented 700,000 who had never heard of her a few weeks before. We surely shall hear of her again, and other women God is raising up as lights in this darkening hour. Barbara herself accurately told why we need modern Deborahs:

"Historically, American women have played a key role in setting the moral tone of our society. The home and the family have been their particular, but by no means exclusive, province. But these traditional sources of our national character have come under corrosive, widespread attack. The women of America are especially motivated to combat and repel that attack.

"Instead, we find most of the advocates of so-called 'women's liberation' serving as routine spokesmen for all the tired causes of the left. Even more appalling, in the name of 'liberation' they press the case for permissiveness or outright immorality, an advocacy directly at odds with the real needs of our times, and the real beliefs of most American women.

"We need liberation from the exhibitionists who misrepresent American women to the nation. We need the special talents and dynamism of the ladies of America to articulate what has been, and remains, right about America . . . .

"In fighting this good fight, we are not abandoning our dedication to our homes and families. Rather, we recognize that dedication is our very first obligation. And we are committed to bring the special insights and abilities of the ladies of America into the public arena, where they are so sorely needed to combat the moral decay that we see rampant in our nation today."

Little did I dream, when I heard those stirring words as well as those of Rita Warren, that I soon would find myself in the public arena. And it all happened in the New York State fight over the innocent-sounding Equal Rights Amendment!

14 *Is God's Way Worth Fighting For?*

Once we crown Jesus as Lord of our lives and determine that His Word will be our "only rule of faith and practice" (the words of the old Westminster Confession), moral and ethical decisions should be "non-negotiable." Yet sometimes there is a strange haziness in God's people. Many are so confused that they defend positions totally contrary to the plain teaching of Scripture.

In recent years we have seen Christians who give lip service to the Bible attack capital punishment, support abortion (which is murder), and defend the so-called Equal Rights Amendment. Such muddled thinking has produced a state of urgent crisis for our nation. DeToqueville once said that democracy carried within itself the seeds of its own ruin. He recognized that once the leadership of our country was no longer just or righteous, and the people indifferent, the end would be in sight.

Like many of my brethren, I have spent most of my Christian life content to leave the "dirty world of politics" to whomever the devil would send in to fill up the gaps. But also like my brethren, I am not content with the *results* of such non-activism. Early Christian patriots like Samuel Adams, if they were walking the earth today, would hang their heads in shame at some of the rest of us. To them, our present dilemma of separating ourselves from the government of our land could only seem a kind of madness. Had our attitude been prevalent in their day, there would have been no American Revolution, nor the freedom they passed on to us as our heritage.

It is high time we "remember the former things." Are we worthy to be the descendants of Pilgrims jammed in the tiny

Mayflower, risking the stormy Atlantic crossing, so that their children might be trained in the Word of God?

Do we have any spiritual kinship with the founders of the "common schools," who saw education's sole purpose to train young people to read and reason according to Scripture?

Can we understand the thinking of evangelical pastors who left their pulpits to fight in the Revolution and frame the Constitution afterward? What did they believe, about which we are hazy?

Congressman John Conlan helped me clear any confusion I may have had on these issues a few weeks ago when I interviewed him for *Christian Life* and my next book on the nation. A born-again, Biblical conservative, the representative from Arizona does not mince words.

"The lines are clearly being drawn these days," he said. "There's a clash between two philosophies of life. One says there is no God—whether outright communism or any of its spinoffs within secular humanism. It has a minor premise: man is good. The other starts with the premise that there is a God: perfect power, perfect love, perfect justice. Its minor premise is that man is imperfect—the sin factor of Romans 3:23.

"Now which way do you go in your theological, secular, political, economic institutions? Do you praise the state? Do you have everyone looking to a centralized government for his salvation?"

These words have rung in my ears the last few weeks as I have seen how accurately he described our present dilemma in the United States. Unwittingly, and I have to admit, almost unwillingly, I have been drawn into the controversy over the Equal Rights Amendment here in New York State. Like so many, for a long time I thought it was nothing but "equal pay for equal work." What a shock it was to discover that the ERA has nothing to do with these rights, already provided for in the Civil Rights Act of 1964 and the Equal Opportunities Act of 1972. What it *does* threaten to do is to bring about a change in our society so radical that it would bear no resemblance to the country once founded by Biblical Christians. Senator Sam Ervin called the ERA "the most drastic measure in Senate history."

Why?

Ironically enough, the very argument women's libbers use as their first to support it provides the greatest hint to what is wrong with it. I have heard several dozen female chauvinists in the past few weeks extol the fact that the Equal Rights Amendment was introduced into Congress every year since 1923. Even a sleepy listener does not have to do very much mental arithmetic to discover that this was very soon after the Bolshevik Revolution, and Lenin's plan to capture the entire world for godless communism. The radical movement in the United States is only a trifle older than the Equal Rights Amendment; they go together as surely as salt and pepper.

The ERA is the masterpiece of the "masters of deceit." Disarming in its simplicity, its very brevity and ambiguity are its most vicious weapons against our Judeo-Christian ethic. It says only that "equality of rights under the law shall not be denied or abridged by the United States or by any state on account of sex."

The Yale Law Journal (April 1971), in its summary on the effects of the ERA on criminal law, said: "Courts faced with criminal laws which do not apply equally to men and women *would be likely to invalidate the laws rather than extending or rewriting them to apply to women and men alike.*"

Thus passage of the ERA would wipe out an avalanche of laws based on the obvious fact, made very clear in Scripture, that men and women are *not* created equal in function, strength, or need for protection. The laws which would rush into oblivion would include certain protections against sexual assault, statutory rape laws, consensual sodomy and adultery laws, and laws designed to protect women from being forced into prostitution.

Yet this danger is but the tip of an iceberg. The really big one is that pinpointed by Congressman Hutchinson of the House Judiciary Committee. He said the ERA "will transfer the power to determine public policy out of the legislative branch and place it in the judiciary—the branch least responsive to the public will . . . . The *language* then becomes the tool of the Supreme Court to interpret at will, and that Court has been known to find meanings and powers in Constitutional amendments undreamed of and unintended by the Congresses which proposed them and the State Legislatures which ratified them."

Commenting on this fact, Rudolph P. Blaum, retired captain of the New York City Police Department, said, "In the light of that observation, with which I wholeheartedly concur, we may be sure that the reference to *sex* in the amendment will not only be interpreted as relating to *gender,* but also as pertaining to *sexual conduct."*

Precisely here this hydra-headed monster rears its ugliest head. Most fervent of all ERA supporters are members of the "gay liberation movement." They hope to bring about a change in our society so complete that Sodom and Gomorrah will have nothing on us. They seek nothing less than homosexual "marriages" and adoption of children—and the right to teach your children and mine—yes, even sex education!

A survey of the homosexual movement was taken by the Brother Collective in Berkeley, California. They reported that 200 groups responded and published the following statement as a result of their findings: "There seems to be a trend, especially on the West Coast, in socialist and feminist direction among anti-sexist men, especially gay men . . . . In the gay movement we see a resurgence of radical activity, reflecting a general deepening and strengthening of leftist organization in this country."

This latter statement also is borne out by several other pertinent facts given very little notice by our average media. FBI Assistant Director W. Raymond Wannall recently reported that Soviet "diplomats" stationed in the United States have doubled since 1968 to a present total of 1,078. Of these, from 70 percent to 80 percent are KGB agents, or have intelligence functions.

Added to these items are facts concerning organizations being funded in pushing the Equal Rights Amendment. *The Los Angeles Times* recently reported that the Rockefeller Foundation gave $288,000 to The President's Advisory Council on the Status of Women (SOW!). Taxpayers' funds in excess of $80,000 also have been appropriated for pro-ERA SOW.

Such money was used to "educate" and influence passage of the amendment, aiding the causes of such radical groups as NOW (the National Organization for Women). The latter group brazenly states its radical design for a new social order in its official publication, *Revolution: Tomorrow is NOW!*

Another interesting source of financial help for ERA is *Playboy* magazine. In the Illinois drive to push the amendment, supporters were allowed to use *Playboy* postal machines for huge mailings, the printed *Playboy* bunny appearing on the envelopes!

There are many other things wrong with the Equal Rights Amendment, such as the fact that it would require women as well as men to be drafted and have an equal chance to become a P.O.W. But it is not my purpose to get into a discussion of those things in this book. Christians need only to know the *source* of a teaching or movement in order to take their stand. The Lord Jesus made it clear that a "good tree cannot produce bad fruit, *nor can a rotten tree produce good fruit*" (Matthew 7:18).

The *source* of the ERA is foul, regardless of how many starry-eyed liberals insist on supporting it. These days when people ask me what the letters ERA stand for, I can answer with no hesitation, "The Evil Rights Amendment!"

Recently New York State has seen an historic controversy over the *state* form of this amendment. In 1972 New York was one of the first states to ratify it for our federal Constitution. This was done with almost no information or debate. Then last year a *state* constitutional amendment was introduced by those too impatient to wait for the federal one to take effect. (Many of us pray it never will, and God is hearing our prayers. Even the *New York Times* conceded recently that the ERA is slipping—an obvious fact, since all but one of the states considering it this year have turned it down at this writing.) Yet some in New York are determined to have mandatory unisex even if the nation rejects it!

Last year the assembly and state senate passed the state amendment quickly—*again* with no debate and hardly a murmur. But Intercessors for America was formed last year (P.O. Box PRAY, Plymouth, Massachusetts, 02360) and has done a good job of informing prayer groups nationwide to pray this thing down. Thus legislators found a more informed public this time. Although the assembly refused to listen to the ground swell against ERA, again passing it, irate wives and mothers statewide protested the steamrolling libbers' cause.

Finally a brave member of the State Senate Judiciary Committee, Senator Bernard Gordon, scheduled public hearings on the ERA. There was almost a virtual media blackout ahead of time, and the hearing was not posted on the regular printed list of hearings. But there were still 500 or so of us there in Albany on March 11. It was an historic occasion. Over 200 had signed up to testify, among them Marge Barnhouse, widow of the late Dr. Donald Grey Barnhouse, and myself.

It was a thrilling day in many ways. Dorothy Frooks, a lawyer who had been a suffragette and who had served in World War I, received a standing ovation at the close of her testimony. A fiery patriot, she warned of the revolutionary goals of the actual framers of the ERA and the total change in our society it would bring about.

I was amazed at the thunderous applause that accompanied my use of the Scriptures: "Woe to those who call evil good, and good evil... who justify the wicked for a bribe, and take away the rights of the ones who are in the right" (Isaiah 5:20, 23).

About two hours later, Marge Barnhouse testified. Her talk was very well received. We also were heartened by the testimony of Jan Hammond who represented the social action committee of the Calvary Baptist Church in New York City. This was a clear implementing of the covenant made at the International Congress on World Evangelization, urging Christian social responsibility.

Following the August 1975 conference, Billy Graham and Bishop Jack Dain were first signers of "The Lausanne Covenant" (signed three hours later by nearly 2000). Article 5 officially removed sanction of our evangelical "ostrich approach" to political and social action, and placed it squarely on the side of becoming involved. It surely is a new day in the world and United States history when contemporary theological conservatives will devote themselves to a purpose like this:

> Here too we express penitence both for our neglect and for having sometimes regarded evangelism and social concern as mutually exclusive. Although reconciliation with man is not reconciliation with God, nor is political liberation salvation, nevertheless *we affirm that evangelism and socio-political involvement are both part of our Christian duty.* (From Article 5 of the Lausanne Covenant, italics added.)

A few weeks before the hearing, I had sat in a legislative forum in Albany listening to two women debate the ERA and observing the furor on the floor, afterward. At that time I slid down in my seat every time the TV cameras went over the audience. My feelings then were positively schizoid! On the one hand I knew I was in the will of God being there, praying and seeking God's will for His people in this thing; on the other hand I was uneasy about being seen by other Christians in the Capital District, thinking I had backslid because I was *there!*

On March 11, all that had changed. Marge and I sat up unashamed as the TV cameras focused on our section of the audience, and many told us later that they saw us that night on the six o'clock news! Between these two occasions I had interviewed Congressman Conlan and renewed my own personal dedication to the principles of the Lausanne Covenant, although I never got a chance to sign it. But most important, the Lord Himself had dealt with me. How would I fare with Him if I tried to argue at the judgment seat of Christ that His "Go ye" could not include the world of politics?

Yet, after I testified one confused woman said she was born again, but believed in the ERA. She told me she objected to my Christian testimony being connected with such an issue, as well as my statement that right and wrong were involved. I tried to show her from the Scriptures that God could never change His standard for roles of the sexes, but quickly found she was not interested.

"I keep *that* part of my life separate from this part," she said.

As she walked away I wondered what the Lord thinks when we dichotomize our lives. Then I remembered Lot's wife. She was so tied to Sodom that she looked back, despite the warning and command of the angels. Thus she became what Lot was called to be in Sodom, but never was—*salt*. Having failed to be the preservative to save their city, he was given a stern and permanent reminder from the Almighty of that disobeyed call. The final act of rationalizing, compromising Lot in the Scriptures was incest with his own daughters (Genesis 19:30-38). Such is the ignominy of those who will not live as overcomers *over* sin; they end up being overcome *by* it.

Noah was different. He must have seemed an oddball to the swingers of his day. Yet with every stroke of the hammer against the planks of gopher wood, his *life* gave ringing affirmation to his faith and verbal testimony. *He was building according to God's Word,* while the world about him spent itself on sin.

The Lord Jesus warned us that the days before His return would be as it was "in the days of Lot" (Luke 17:28) and "in the days of Noah" (Matthew 24:37). Lot never lived convincingly enough among his family to win them all to the Lord; *Noah's whole family was saved when God destroyed the world around them.*

What will it be like with us? How will we and our families behave in the final battles between light and darkness in this age? Are we taking seriously God's plan of total saturation of His Word for all of us?

> "Hear, O Israel! The Lord is our God, the Lord is one! And you shall love the Lord your God with all your heart and with all your soul, and with all your might. And these words, which I am commanding you today, shall be on your heart; and you shall teach them diligently to your sons and shall talk of them when you sit in your house and when you walk by the way and when you lie down and when you rise up. And you shall bind them as a sign on your hand and they shall be as frontals on your forehead. And you shall write them on the doorposts of your house and on your gates." (Deuteronomy 6:4-9).

> "Let the word of Christ richly dwell within you; with all wisdom teaching and admonishing one another with psalms and hymns and spiritual songs, singing with thankfulness in your hearts to God." (Colossians 3:16.)

We had better do it *now*. Behind the Iron and Bamboo Curtains, where personal and religious freedom already are gone, the only Bible many Christians have is that written on their hearts. Our own prisoners of war, returning from North Vietnam, gave moving testimony to the power of the Word of God. Some men endured solitary confinement for more than four years. Many were tortured. They stayed sane only through remembering portions of Scripture from childhood days. These they tapped out to one another in code on the walls between their cells, often suffering as a result of doing so. Most of these men deplored the fact that they had learned so little Scripture before they went into captivity. Can we listen to their testimonies unmoved?

The Lord Jesus Christ never intended that His end-time people sit on their back porch waiting for the Rapture! No, He said, "Do business with this until I come back" (Luke 19:13). *His way of looking up was on the fields white unto harvest, not for a way of escape from anything unpleasant to Western hedonism.*

Will it take the smoldering rubble from incinerated cities to convince us God wants disciples, not Disney characters? Must we stand in fields of browning stubble during famine to see that God needs good Samaritans, not grandiose charlatans? Shall we "preserve the unity of the Spirit in the bond of peace," or will Christ face us at His judgment seat with others in His family we dared to ignore?

The time when our primary concern is our own individual needs and problems—even *family* needs and problems—is nearly over. God wants every child of the King putting on the whole armour of God, prepared for the final confrontation with the forces of darkness.

Deborah was not too squeamish to go to battle against the enemy that would destroy God's people. She was willing to respond to God's call, through His servant Barak, to aid His armies in war. When we last see her in Scripture she is singing God's praises because His people are functioning as they should:

> "That the *leaders led* in Israel,
> That the *people volunteered*,
> Bless the Lord!" (Judges 5:2).

We search in vain through the divine record for censure of her or others who used their abilities and means for God's glory. Yet we do find condemnation for the one with a talent who judged his lord to be a hard and cruel man, and so hid what he had, accomplishing nothing (Matthew 25:24-30).

What do *you* think of your Lord, today? Down through the ages His eternal question rings, "What do you think about the Christ?" (Matthew 22:42.)

Do you see Him as He is—loving, kind, and of infinite mercy to those who believe Him and obey His Word? Do you realize He has given you what you have to use for Him? Can you hide it in the ground (or in the bank) and still have peace about facing Him? Remember, "He died for all, that they who live should *no longer live for themselves,* but for Him who died and rose again on their behalf" (II Corinthians 5:15).

What does this mean, in practical terms? How different are lives ignited by the Holy Spirit for service?

Very different. Our lives soar as eagles far above the mole-like existence of those who burrow in the darkness of their own selfishness and introversion. Liberated from problem-centeredness, we fly on wings of prayer and praise through jet streams of joy. Living above circumstances—even bad ones—we maintain our perspective. And we submit these to the anvil of God's dealings so that He may fashion from them something useful for His glory.

For such lives, Acts 1:8 becomes a promise ever-reaching out to more vistas of fulfillment. We let our light shine first in our homes and churches: our Jerusalems. Then we reach out to our whole area: those Judaeas where we work and study and have a civic concern. Nor can we forget the Samarias—those places we would rather not go—bus ministry to the ghettos, pornography and textbook controversies, sex education battles, and the myriad of other challenges which break the heart of a holy God who also is Love.

With hearts burning in an ever-widening witness for Jesus Christ, it is only normal then to reach out to the uttermost parts of the earth. Our wallets and formerly wasted moments become the secret citadels of lives burning on the altar of the Great Commission. Hands stretched over the pages of an atlas wet with our tears carry us to any corner of the world where God needs prayer.

Doubtless there will be some who will say, "But why all the urgency? What's the great rush?"

The answer to that question can be found in a recent message by Corrie ten Boom, author of *The Hiding Place,* from which the Billy Graham Association film (with the same title) was made:

"In China the Christians were told, 'Don't worry, before the tribulation comes, you will be translated—raptured.' Then came a terrible persecution. Millions of Christians were tortured to death. Later I heard a Bishop from China say sadly, 'We have failed. We should have made the people strong for persecution rather than telling them Jesus would come first.'

"Turning to me, he said, 'You still have time. Tell the people how to be strong in times of persecution, how to stand when the tribulation comes—to stand and not faint.' "

Did not the King show His daughter these things so that others of His sons and daughters might redeem the time *now?*

How will it be with you?

"Choose for yourselves this day whom you will serve" (Joshua 24:15).

BIBLIOGRAPHY

Books:

Bennett, Rita. *I'm Glad You Asked That.* Edmonds, Wash./Plainfield, N.J.: Aglow/Logos, 1974.
Brooks, Pat. *Climb Mount Moriah.* Monroeville, Pa.: Whitaker House, 1974.
Brooks, Pat. *Out! In the Name of Jesus.* Carol Stream, Ill.: Creation House, 1972.
Brooks, Pat. *Using Your Spiritual Authority.* Monroeville, Pa.: Whitaker House, 1973.
Buess, Bob. *The Pendulum Swings.* Indianola, Iowa: Inspirational Marketing, Inc., 1974.
Christensen, Larry. *The Christian Family.* Minneapolis, Minn.: Bethany Fellowship, 1970.
Derstine, Gerald, *Women's Place in the Church.* Bradenton, Fla.: Harvest Time, no date.
Hunt, Gladys. *Ms. Means Myself.* Grand Rapids Mich.: Zondervan Corp., 1972.
Lovett, C.S. *The Divorce Problem.* Baldwin Park, Calif.: Personal Christianity, 1959. *The Compassionate Side of Divorce,* 1975.
Lovett, C.S. *Unequally Yoked Wives.* Baldwin Park, Calif.: Personal Christianity, 1968.
Renich, Jill. *To Have and To Hold.* Grand Rapids, Mich.: Zondervan Corp., 1972.
Warren, Rita. *Mom, They Won't Let Us Pray.* Westwood, N.J.: Fleming H. Revell Company, 1975.

Periodicals:

Christian Life Magazine, Gundersen Drive and Schmale Road, Wheaton, Ill., 60187.

Human Events, 422 First Street, S.E., Washington, D.C., 20003.
Phyliss Schafly Report, Box 618, Alton, Ill., 62002.
U.S. News & World Report, 2300 N. Street, N.W., Washington, D.C., 20037.